Jürgen Kriz: S

GW00871395

This book is dedicated to

Carl R. Rogers

psychologist,
known as the originator of the

Person-Centered Approach

and

Hermann Haken

physicist,
known as the founder of

Synergetics

two people, who indescribably
challenged my thinking

JÜRGEN KRIZ

SELF-
ACTUALIZATION

For Rachael
with all my good wishes
to follow further the
track of longing for understanding
"the world" — i.e. relations to
the universe, other people and
last but not least to you
yourself

Warmly

Saas Fee, 7'2010

Bibliographische Information Der Deutschen Bibliothek:

Die Deutsche Bibliothek verzeichnet diese Publikation in der
Deutschen Nationalbibliographie; detaillierte bibliographische
Daten sind im Internet über < http://dnb.ddb.de abrufbar

ISBN 3–8334–5255–2

Herstellung und Verlag: Books on Demand GmbH
Norderstedt

CONTENTS

Preface

Over the last years, colleagues and friends have encouraged me to translate more of my writing into the English language. Indeed, compared to my publications in the German language, my complete works from the perspective of an (only) English-speaking reader are extremely small—hardly a dozen papers and book chapters. Moreover, some are in volumes addressed more to colleagues from the natural sciences or systems theoretic psychology. And that is hardly something that therapists, for example, want to read.

This book now contains seven chapters based on the translations of papers focusing on the concept of self-actualization. I chose this term—an alternative to "self-organization"—in order to particularly address the work to people interested in and influenced by Carl Rogers' person-centered approach to psychotherapy. Moreover, the preference for "self-actualization" should make it clear that processes of self-organization in the context of matter or even biology are not our concern in this book.

Admittedly, examples from those fields of study will be used to explain some essential principles. This is due to the fact that these examples can be treated and discussed in a much more isolated way, and are therefore "simple" compared with the much greater complexity of the cognitive and interactive processes of human beings.

However, understanding some *principles* by way of examples from the natural sciences does not at all entail the reduction of psychological and social *phenomena* and processes to natural science. For example, we could use the process of growth in a deciduous tree to explain that the *principle* of "growth" in humanistic psychology does not mean "more and more" (as is in economics) but "die and become" in adaptation to the changing environment (here: the seasons). However, this does not mean that I want to reduce personal growth to biological phenomena.

I hope this remark prevents any misunderstanding regarding the intention of this book.

Focusing on self-actualization only rather implicitly hints at some ideas of a broader approach that I have been working on for more than two decades, which I called "Person centered Systems Theory". The work needed for an adequate translation of papers directly addressed to that context would have gone far beyond the capacities of this project. However, I don't see a problem in accepting constraints. On the contrary, every paper or book is meant as an invitation for a cognitive encounter. I wonder who will feel invited.

Writing in a foreign language or translating well elaborated descriptions and argumentations into another language is hard work. I am very grateful for the extensive help given by Colleen Beaumont, Henry D. Cooke, and Cliodhna Quigley. Special thanks also to the students of the "European Graduate School" (EGS), Saas Fee, Switzerland, with whom I was able to discuss provisional drafts of some English papers, as well as to my colleagues from the EGS faculty, particularly Majken Jacoby from Denmark.

May this book contribute to the task of providing psychologists and psychotherapists with more adequate concepts and metaphors for an understanding of the intra- and interpersonal processes of human beings than the inadequate metaphors and principles of mechanistic science.

June, 2006   Jürgen Kriz

Introduction

Is there a difference between beating out the dents in a tin can or repairing a defective engine, and making an intervention with a living being or even working with a patient in a psychotherapeutic manner?

Most people, and not just advocates of humanistic psychology, would agree with and plead for such a difference. Some would even add that this difference is essential.

But what are the concepts, terms, metaphors and principles that we have and use as cognitive tools to grasp, explain and discuss human development, pathogenesis or psychotherapy? After 400 years of great success on the part of the classical mechanistic science as an essential basis of today's culture, our world is filled with machines, apparatus, tools, and "things", and has changed the face of our planet. Over many generations, our inner images—the metaphors and principles we use in understanding our every-day life—became, of course, more and more related to the outer images of what we perceive and experience: things and mechanical apparatus (and consequently, the effective handling of rather complicated machines is reduced in our every-day world to the operation of simple mechanical apparatus, for example to press a knob, to flick a switch and so on).

No wonder then that it seemed self-evident to use these metaphors and principles to understand and explain other areas of the "world"—when we are dealing with living beings, with other humans and last but not least with our-selves. This tendency seems to be even stronger when we try to give rational or "scientific" explanations. Although modern science has changed its world view and its ex-planatory principles tremendously, the informal narra-tives and metaphors of culture don't adapt as quickly, but instead still convey the "same old stories" of what "sci-ence" is. And this still involves the use of a toolbox of mechanistic principles (which are indeed rather adequate in dealing with the restricted apparatus of our technical world).

Moreover, the world view of modern science is rather anti-intuitive, highly sophisticated—expressed in the main by differential equations and even more compli-cated mathematical tools. In short, this new world view is a "closed session" of scientists and is and will be very slow to change the classical ideology.

As a consequence, the *knowledge* that there is an es-sential difference between an engine and a human being and the *will* to adequately respect this are not enough to effect a change, if we still use the cognitive tools from mechanistic science. Even in the writings and sayings of humanistic therapists, we find many mechanistic meta-phors that allude more to the principles of flattening a dented tin can than of facilitating the self-organized tran-sition of an ailing structure of life-processes to a more satisfying one.

I want to further elucidate this point by discussing one aspect.

We have clear terms to refer to somebody's change from "being healthy" to the "state" of "being ill", for ex-ample "pathogenesis". Similarly, we have clear terms for referring to the opposite situation—somebody's change from "being ill" to the "state" of "being healthy", for example "therapy". In general, such clear terms always correspond to the main topics of explanation in active areas of discussion. And indeed, we do want to explain why "things" are changing and who or what has made the change. If a dented tin can is suddenly in good shape again, we ask who did it and how he did it. In contrast, if the can remains in its former state (considered over a reasonable time-frame), nothing seems to need to be explained. Things don't change until somebody changes them. And it's for this reason that we don't have and don't need terms to describe the absence of change.

However, focusing on the *processes* of life change is natural and normal. You cannot step into the same river twice, because neither the river nor you are exactly the same and, moreover, the experience of the "first time" is lost. Therefore, in the stream of moments of an ever changing world of processes, we don't so much need to explain "change", but rather "no-change" or stability.

What are the cognitive and linguistic "tools" that we use to conceptually and terminologically refer to this phenomenon of "no-change"? In the case of being healthy, the term "salutogenesis" has been around for some years, but it's so brand-new that many people haven't heard of it at all. But how to refer to being (and staying!) "pathological"?

I personally don't know of any term, although in the last hundred years since Sigmund Freud, nearly all psychotherapists have stressed the point that symptoms can be equated with the absence of the ability to change and to adapt to new tasks and requirements. In general, if there is no term available to describe a particular phenomenon, this is a pretty good sign that it is not important in the discourses. And this again indicates that in our reifying culture the tin-can-metaphor is more typical than the idea of processes.

Self-actualization, the title of this book, refers to a core concept both in Carl Rogers' person-centered approach to psychotherapy and in modern systems theory. Rogers took this term from theoretical approaches which are in line with modern systems theory (for example Gestalt and organismic theory). Moreover, he was one of very few psychologists who were aware of the rise of modern systems theory which supported his conceptions, for example Ilia Prigogine's Nobel-prize win in chemistry 1977 for his "dissipative structures" (a special version of self-organization theory).

However, even many psychologists and therapists claiming themselves to be in accordance with the person-centered approach did not understand this essential principle for a long time (and some don't even today) and preferred just to use the therapeutic procedures and, at best, the "philosophy" of a personal relationship. Thus weakened, the person-centered approach wasn't able to offensively defend its essential principles in the highly competitive area of psychotherapeutic approaches, which was influenced by the forces of an increasing reductionism towards genetic explanations and medical treatments.

In this book, I want to discuss the idea of self-actualization in the context of different themes. The intention is to provide the reader with thoughts, ideas, metaphors and knowledge which are more adequate to understand processes of life—especially on the cognitive and interactional level. First, some additional clarification of the term "self-actualization" should be given:

Self-actualization has a double meaning, which is due to the different uses of the word "self".

Firstly, "self-actualization" refers to the universal phenomenon that a system, particularly an organism, need not be "formed", "ordered" or structured" by an "organizer" which integrates the elements into an organized whole. Instead, given an appropriate environment, it will unfold itself in an orderly way. This was stressed, among others, by the Gestalt psychologist Kurt Goldstein (1878 – 1965), who, after his emigration to the USA, became more famous as an "organismic theorist".[1]

Therefore *the term "self" in "self-actualization" functions as a terminological focus on "self-made" in contrast to "made from outside".*

Of course, Goldstein and other organismic theorists did not mean that the organism is immune to the events and forces of the external world. Conversely, the environment is both a source of supplies and disturbances with which the organism must cope. For example, Goldstein wrote:

The tasks are determined by the "nature" of the organism, its "essence", which is brought into actualization through environmental changes that act upon it. The expressions of that actualization are the performances of the organism. Through them the organism can deal with the respective environmental demands and actualize itself." (1939, p. 111) Therefore, the healthy organism is one "in which the tendency towards self-actualization is acting from within, and overcomes the disturbance arising from the clash with the world" (1939, p. 305).

It is fascinating how much this notion and world view corresponds with the thoughts of modern interdisciplinary systems theory, which appeared in the natural sciences more than three decades after the publication of Gold-

---

[1] like Ludwig von Bertalanffy (1901-1972), known for his general systems theory or Andras Angyal (1902-1960), known for the "biosphere".

stein's fundamental book "The Organism" (1939, German edition 1934).[2]

In modern systems theory, "self-organization" refers to the phenomenon that a system organizes itself due to inner structural possibilities (in relation to the environment but not structurally enslaved by it). Moreover, when Goldstein talks about the "re-organization" of old patterns into new and more effective or better adapted patterns, this is exactly what we mean by "phase transition" in modern systems theory. In particular, the interdisciplinary approach of "Synergetics" by Hermann Haken provides a conceptual basis and framework for facilitating cooperations between those psychologists and natural scientists who are interested in understanding complex autonomous (but not isolated or immune) processes of self-organized order.

Secondly, the term "self-actualization" is a core concept in the "person-centered" (or "client-centered") approach to psychotherapy developed by Carl R. Rogers (1902-1987). However, Rogers was also a famous theorist of personality and his elaborated self theory in particular is cited by many psychologists. For example, 50 years ago the handbook on "Theories of Personality" by Hall and Lindzey included a chapter on Rogers' self theory, stating "Rogers' theory on personality represents a synthesis of phenomenology as presented by Snygg and Combs, of holistic and organismic theory as developed in the writings of Goldstein, Maslow, and Angyal, of Sullivan's interpersonal theory, and of self theory for which

---

[2] Of course there were always similar holistic and systemic thoughts in our and in other cultures, before and after Goldstein. I want to at least mention the collaboration between the psychologist C.G. Jung and the Nobel-physicist Wolfgang Pauli on "archetypes" which, partly even in the mathematical details, anticipated concepts that came up (again) in the discourses of systems theory decades later—cf. Kriz 1998

Rogers himself is largely responsible..." (Hall and Lindzey 1957, p. 478).

Unlike Goldstein, who wasn't interested in an explicit and particular self-theory, the "self" as a nuclear concept in Rogers' theory of personality is a differentiated object of discourse. In a series of nineteen propositions, formulated in "Client-centered Therapy" (1951), Rogers states: "8. A portion of the total perceptual field gradually becomes differentiated as the self" and "9. As a result of interaction with the environment, and particularly as a result of evaluational interactions with others, the structure of the self is formed—an organized, fluid, but constant conceptual pattern of perceptions of characteristics and relationships of the 'I' or the 'me' together with the values attached to these concepts".

Psychopathology is understood to result from an "incongruence" of the organismic experiences and their symbolization by the self, due to introjections—according to Rogers "values introjected or taken over from others, but perceived in a distorted fashion, as if they had been experienced directly." As a consequence, some experiences may be "ignored because there is no perceived relationship to the self-structure" or "denied symbolization or given a distorted symbolization because the experience is inconsistent with the structure of the self".

Therefore, for Rogers the distinction between the human organism—which is the total individual and the basis for the totality of experience (the phenomenal field) —and the self—which is a differentiated, structured portion of this field—is essential.

In Rogers' theory, the organizational development of the human organism is understood in accordance with the organismic theorists to be autonomous (but not isolated or immune) and is called "actualization". Additionally, Rogers calls the organizational development of the self, also understood to be autonomous (but not isolated or immune), "self-actualization".

Therefore, in Rogers' theory, *the term "self" in "self-actualization" functions as a terminological focus on the "self" in contrast to the totality of experience or the "actualization" of the organism.*

Of course, actualizing a "self" by means of self-actualization is he typical and essential capability of the actualization of the human organism in contrast to the actualization of the organisms of animals or plants (which do not, as far as we know today, develop a "self").

As already mentioned, the term "self" in the interdisciplinary discourses on "self-organization" refers to the first meaning, i.e. it stresses the aspect of being ordered and organized by itself and not by an "organizer" which imposes order from outside the system. From this perspective, the actualization of the organism is, of course, due to self-organization (as the organismic theorists had already said). Moreover, the actualization of the "self" can also be understood by way of self-organization of cognitive processes.[3]

---

[3] This, of course leads to a terminological Problem. From the perspective of systems theory, therefore, Rogers "self-actualization" means "self"-self-organization. This is, of course, a strange and complicated term. Whenever this problem occurs we should therefore replace "self-organization" with "automorphism" (a term which was already used in the dialog between C.G. Jung and Wolfgang Pauli, because the term "self-organization" wasn't in the scientific discourses and Pauli, therefore, referred to the work of the famous French mathematicians Poincarè, Julia and Fatou who developed the fundamentals of systems and chaos theory five to eight decades before the Americans Edward Lorenz or Benoit Mandelbrot, in ignorance of European thought, re-detected and re-developed chaos-theory, fractal geometry and so on).

Instead of self-self-organization we should speak of "self"-automorphism.

It should be clear that this terminological problem occurs not only with respect to person-centered theory, but also in many psychological

In this book, however, I have tried to avoid these terminological problems. In many cases the phenomena are dealt with in a rather general manner by using therefore the neutral term "self-organization". However, the reader with an interest in therapeutic aspects is asked to fill out these descriptions with his knowledge and experience concerning self-actualization and actualization of the "self".

References

Bertalanffy, L. von (1950) An outline of general systems theory. Brit. J. Phil.Sci. 134-165

Goldstein, K. (1939) The Organism. New York: American Book. (German edition 1934: Der Aufbau des Organismus, Den Haag)

Hall, C. S. & Lindzey G. (1957) Theories of Personality. New York: Wiley

Haken, H. (1978) Synergetics. An Introduction. Nonequilibrium Phase Transitions in Physics, Chemistry and Bilogy. Berlin-New York: Springer

Haken, H. (1983) Advanced synergetics. Instability Hierarchies. Berlin-New York: Springer

---

texts which refer both to the interdisciplinary discourse on self-organization and to the "self" as a psychological construct. For example, in many psychological texts talking about "self-regulation", "self-development" and so on, I feel confused and lost by the question of whether the author is talking about something that means "auto"-regulation or "auto"-development (stressing the autonomous aspects), or if he wants to discuss the regulation or the development of the "self" as a psychological construct.

Kriz, J. (1998) Archetypische Ordnungen. Die Begegnung von Physik und Psychotherapie. In: "Vom Sinn im Zufall. Anregungen von Wolfgang Pauli aus seinem Dialog mit C.G.Jung" Evangelische Akademie Mülheim/ Ruhr

Rogers, C.R. (1951). The Client-centered therapy; its current practice, implications, and theory. Boston: Houghton

Chapter 1

MY THEORETICAL ORIENTATION
AND ITS UNDERLYING PATH OF LIFE

In 2003 I was invited to contribute a chapter to a book edited by Otto F. Kernberg, Birger Dulz and Jochen Eckert, in which psychotherapists talk about themselves and their "impossible" profession. Although the range of topics and titles was rather wide, I was asked to write this very personal chapter. For a long time I was quite hesitant to publish such private thoughts—not least because of the usual valid reserve found in the academic world. However, some friends encouraged me (and some did not!) and finally I decided to do it this way. One reason was that, anyhow, my papers and books made it increasingly clear anyway that I cannot report anything about "the world", but only about my personal encounters with the world (not only according to the humanistic and systemic-constructivistic point of view but also according to famous natural scientists. For example, as Werner Heisenberg, winner of the Nobel Prize for Physics, stated 50 years ago: "When we talk nowadays about the world-view of the exact natural sciences, we no longer refer to a picture of nature, but to a picture of our relationship to nature"). The other reason was that I find it helpful for readers, colleagues and students to know a little more about the underlying path of life corresponds to the (stand)point that was reached (or rather that has been reached until now) along the way, in order to gain a deeper understanding of the perspective related to that point of view.

This is also the reason why I start this book with a description based on a translation of that very book chapter.

Faced with the challenging incredible complexity of "the world" (meaning the abundance of human experiences based on encounter of man with nature, man and himself), every single theory, concept(ion), practice, and concrete act is associated with certain decisions to implement necessary limitations. These limitations reflect the answers we give to the general questions of what we consider to be important.

This statement seems to be part of a rather abstract consideration in the philosophy of science. However, for me personally, it has an enormously relevant meaning for my life. Since my earliest childhood, and on into my earliest memories, these limitations occurred to me in the form of a deep longing to overcome the borders of my experience and of my expressive possibilities. As a child, I had already painfully experienced and realized my ignorance of a multitude of fascinating phenomena, and of the impossibility to get to the very depth of these phenomena. And none of this improved in any way along the path from schoolboy to student to professor—conversely, the space occupied by the things I didn't know, and by my lack of understanding and explanation expanded faster than that taken up by continuing insights, and this expansion seems to continue without end.

Of course, psychoanalytic and rational categorization can give some context to this experience—for instance, that it was more or less a large "childish" fantasy of omnipotence that was reflected in this pain, and that this longing has a corresponding biographical aspect. For example, my father was called back to the WWII front shortly after my birth, never to return, which meant that my mother had to bring up three children during the post-war confusion almost completely without support. This often brought her to the limits of her abilities—and trained my sensitivity to the needs and feelings of others.

However, such explanatory framing only slightly changes the experience itself. Moreover, I don't even know if I really want to change it—I experience this insatiable desire not only as also a deficiency but also as a great source of energy along my path of life. The compulsion to transcend the boundaries of my all too narrow knowledge and insight deprives me of sleep from time to time, and becomes an almost addictive yearning. When this affects my health too much, I sometimes envy those colleagues who can carry on their scientific work with a fixed rhythm, in the same way as office workers, managing to simply down their cognitive tools in the evening, on weekends and during holidays.

Looking back from my current theoretical perspective, I would say that my path of life was always characterized by a deep fascination for "chaos" (see Kriz 1997). For me, the complexity of the phenomena that are open to experience in their unique configuration in the here and now was always an essential aspect of my Lebenswelt. The sensory experience of the performance of a symphony—Mahler's Third, for instance—and the simultaneous awareness that these notes played by these musicians for this audience constitute a part of a situation that is always unique, has often given me a reverent shiver. And I was all too often aware of the inadequacy of the reductions that are necessary in order to capture such unique sensory complexity in the form of repeatable, abstract categories.

Plenty of lucky coincidences were important for my path. My choice of subjects at high school had me set for a career as a musician, but thankfully I recognized and accepted my limits shortly before beginning my university studies, and I then chose Psychology as my major. However, the role of "musician" at a high school where music was highly valued granted me certain "artistic" liberties, and meant that the usually primarily repetitive transfer of knowledge was a moderately relevant "disturbance" during my learning experiences there. After that, as a university student and young scientist, I had the great luck to meet teachers who thought in such a complex way themselves that my thoughts were not mutilated into "true" knowledge by means of the usual trivializations, indoctrinations and categorical reductions of a university education. Those whom I now hold to be most significant are exactly the people who instilled in me a distrust of "truths". They taught me the unimportance of accomplished rote-learning of books and repeating the content parrot-fashion, and facilitated a trust in my own thinking and cognitive work. This means above all else that one can enter into new perspectives by critical scrutiny. This is one of the most important things I've learned, and something I also try to pass on to my own students.

The "Institute for Advanced Studies" in Vienna (Austria), which I originally wanted to attend for two weeks to learn programming when I was a student, and where I was then allowed to stay for over three years, was a further stroke of luck. I benefited from the tremendous freedom at the institute, the opportunity to work together with famous scientists from all over the world, and even more, to be paid for all of this. One of the more far-reaching pieces of good fortune, which later determined my path of life more than anything I had actually planned, was that I took Astronomy and Astrophysics as a joint major along with my Psychology studies. This led to over a decade of work in methodologies at university departments of sociology and social science. After this, already a full Professor of Statistics, Research Methods and Philosophy of Science in Osnabrück, I again re-oriented myself, beginning a training in psychotherapy. The final big coincidence on my path of realization was just as unexpected as it was lucky; after some years of treating my therapeutic work as a "second job" to my professorship in methods, I was finally able to change it to a "main job" in 1981, as a Professor for Psychotherapy and Clinical Psychology (or, to be more precise, in 1999, when the title of my Chair was officially changed).

It is clear that such a journey through life acts as an immunization against any possible restrictions on one's experiences and thinking by the limitations of therapeutic schools, or by the same token by scientific schools and belief systems. The many years and discussions in co-operation with natural scientists on the one hand and social scientists on the other made it impossible for me to share in the arrogance of many psychologists regarding the "inexact" nature of discourse in the social sciences (considered by some psychologists to be littered with nonsensical ideas).

In addition, I was also unable to share in the extremely naive fixation on the "natural scientific" perspective—a perspective that seems to be almost entirely limited to the Weltbild which was characteristic of Western natural science at the end of the 19th century. This is true, however, only in the long run. To be honest, I have to admit that I also reacted with defensive arrogance at first, when, after studying experimentally oriented Psychology (and a second major of Astronomy) and working in a more computing and mathematically oriented department in Vienna, I suddenly moved to the Department of Social Sciences at the University of Hamburg. (This move was quite unexpected for me—shortly before I was to take up a position at the Institute of Psychology, the position it-self was cancelled during the upheaval of university and educational politics of 1970. The sociologists were part of the same faculty, heard about the problem, and offered me an equivalent position).

The change to Sociology was like entering another world, where the language, structures, and even the prob-lems were completely alien to me at first. My heavily hostile defense reaction, which manifested as a large bias towards devaluing reactions, later served as a warning ex-ample for me. In spite of my desire for knowledge and insight, I was still too unsure of myself to encounter these foreign parts called "sociology" without psychological arrogance—especially when faced with the threat of a complete confusion of my world view.

Today, I see that challenge as a blessing, because my extremely narrow "scientific" perspective—in the form of a cognitive stovepipe—was forced open. I'm not really sure whether this narrow-mindedness, which resulted from a thorough yet one-sided academic training, would still have opened up if this confrontation hadn't taken place—in other words, whether my "youthful folly" at the start of my academic career would have simply been automatically decreased in order to make space for more wisdom (or, at the very least, for knowledge of other po-sitions and viewpoints). It seems to me that especially those academic careers which are based on a more so-phistical level of thinking and method lead to an acade-mic view that contracts as it deepens, and the final result is a loss of an overall picture.

I therefore completely understand why particularly those psychologists who are well grounded and best trained in their paradigm can show a similar ignorance and condescension towards other scientific positions during today's academic and professional political discus-sions. Nevertheless, I often feel furious when faced with the impudence which is used to propagate an often extremely restricted viewpoint as "the science", while simultaneously denying and devaluing all other scientific perspectives. My feelings result from the powerlessness to respond in a similarly efficient way to the enormous efficiency of this intelligent yet limited view of the world. People who don't question their own position and who take their own perspective as the only "true" or correct one, promoting their own procedure as "science" while discrediting other positions, perspectives, and procedures as "unscientific" or "false", don't need to waste any time critically reflecting upon their own point of view.

For such people, there is no point in asking the question of how these so-called "truths" and "scientific" results could possibly look from another perspective, and to ask whether they remain invariant over all alternative points of view and methods. No time has to be spent in discussion with the perspectives and arguments of any other position because their unscientific (mis-)labeling renders any debate unnecessary. In short, such people can devote the entirety of their time and energy to their supposed truth (and to being socially endorsed by the other followers of their view). This position is therefore not only hugely powerful in itself; rather, it is something that is acutely desired and ultimately favorable in our society, which has been made increasingly insecure by a growing complexity of international economic, administrative and media worlds, and which is thus desirous of simple "truths" in which people can believe.

Although much on my path of life was already laid out by these lucky coincidences, the development of my theoretical perspective in the clinical-therapeutic field also had a particular point of culmination. Because my change to a Professorship in Psychotherapy happened at a reasonably late stage, I felt the need to make my way through the mass of published knowledge in this area. It was quite a lucky circumstance that I was far from the beginning of an academic career. I was professionally established and had a considerable amount of books and other publications to my name (even if they were extensively methodological, statistical, and theoretical scientific in their content). This meant that I could distance myself from all the superficialities of academia, like diligence and probationary terms, and get to work - although the (at first under-estimated) demands of time, as well as health and social limitations would certainly prevent me from once more embarking on such an undertaking. For each of the main therapeutic approaches, my work strategy was to read as much material for as long as was needed to become completely convinced of that approach.

This was an unbelievably enriching challenge—also for my prejudices. It increased my respect for the achievements of the founders of these schools of thought, almost all of whom endeavored—in an intellectually honest way—to systematize and structure their extensive clinical-therapeutic experiences and knowledge in such a way that it became communicable. At the end of this work, I was (and am) completely convinced by more than a dozen "approaches" (depending on the inclusive or divisive method of counting). This didn't seem possible to me unless I had arrived at a point of view that integrated these different positions enough to allow the reconstruction of their essential aspects. And so a concept arose that would some years later be called "Person-Centered System Theory".

Admittedly, as stated earlier, substantial reductions are also a necessary aspect of an integrative theoretical position, in that certain decisions must be made regarding the central perspectives. It seems to me that an orientation in systems theory, especially one based on the concepts of Synergetics, is a particularly fruitful starting point. Synergetics is an interdisciplinary theory of self-organization, which in particular explains the connection between micro and macro processes, questions of stability and instability, as well as the self-organizing emergence and transition of dynamic structures. This accommodates the requirements needed for an understanding of psychotherapy (and psychopathology), because a psychotherapeutic theory should account for processes and their interactions on the physical, mental, and social levels at the very least.

The self-organization of dynamic structures in particular is a very suitable model for the explanation of clinical-therapeutic processes. The observable expressions of the individual processes of living—like speech, behavior, and action—are certainly influenced by physical, biological and social laws, but they are in no way determined by these laws, and are thus understandable as self-organizing. Similarly, we observe certain regularities in the interactions of couples, families, and groups. These regularities must also be understood as self-organizing—although legal, biological, or individual behavioral "laws" do indeed play a role, they certainly don't fully determine the specific structures that emerge.

The particular focus on the procedural aspect necessitates the explanation not only of the changes involved —meaning the *transitions* from "healthy" to "sick" (i.e. "pathology") and "sick" to "healthy" (i.e."therapy"). Rather, the *stability* involved must also be explained—why does someone remain "healthy" or "sick"? This functional view of "sickness" and its symptoms has always been an important subject of discussion in psychotherapy—it is the non-adaptiveness of the dynamic life structures to changes in surrounding or contextual conditions which leads to the need for therapy. For example, consider a certain organizational structure of a couple with a three year old child. Although this structure may work well in these circumstances, if it remains unchanged twenty years later when the child is 23, then it is judged to be pathological. Other typical phenomena of systems theory also correspond very well to therapeutic experiences—including the non-linearity of personality changes in the process of psychotherapy (qualitative leaps), and the consideration of the respective stage and state of this process. In systems theory the "same" intervention has different effects depending on the history and the current state of the system.

In spite of the usefulness of a systems theoretical perspective and its advantages (for example, to connect psychotherapy more easily to interdisciplinary discourses), in my point of view, this scientific approach alone does not suffice. The essence of man, in the Heideggerian sense, is that man cannot be understood as a category or class like all other "things" of this world which are defined by their "whatness". "But man is never a what—his essence (self) lies in his existence", as King (1964) stressed. Man, as a reflexive being, can—and must—meaningfully define his existence and his presence in this world. The different modes of being himself free him from categorization.

From this point of view, a person can only be grasped "from the inside"—through his personal understanding and narratives of his biographical past, his meaning and value structures, as well as his ideas of his future. Psychology is exactly the science, which must face both of these perspectives—a science, therefore, in which the inner and outer views of the processes of life meet.

This is also one of the reasons why I have made so much effort to plead for the retention of a multitude of different therapeutic approaches, while advancing my work towards a single comprehensive theory of psychotherapeutic (and psychopathological) processes, from which the different approaches can be reconstructed as extensively as possible. However, this call for a holistic theoretical approach is contrary to the trend of the time to unify therapeutic *practice* as well. The multitude of psychotherapeutic practices is namely a result of the fact that therapists, like patients, are members of a society which is not completely forced into line, but rather contains a variety of values, lifestyles and goals, preferences and ways of viewing the world.

I don't want to provide my patients, and myself, with a theory (and corresponding therapeutic treatment) that doesn't adequately take into account people's curiosity and desire for insight, as well as the differences in their lifestyles and values. I don't want a theory regulated by means of a reduction to a few predetermined standard solutions and allegedly "scientifically validated" generally binding "truths". It is for this reason that I have been pleading for many years for a complex holistic theory with complementary internal and external perspectives, and a diversity of practical therapeutic approaches with their many different "Menschenbilder" and their many different ways of proceeding.

References

King, Magda (1964): Heideggers Philosophy. New York: Macmillan Co.

Kriz, Jürgen (1997): Chaos, Angst und Ordnung. Wie wir unsere Lebenswelt gestalten. Göttingen/Zürich: Vandenhoeck & Ruprecht (Chaos, Fear and Order. How we shape our Lebenswelt.)

Chapter 2

ON CHAOS AND ORDER

A decade ago, I was working on a book on systems theory for psychologists, psychotherapists and doctors (the first edition appeared 1997). I liked that book, which was meant as a fundamental textbook bringing some of the core ideas of modern systems thinking to the "clinical field". Although it was addressed much more to clinical problems than another book which I wrote five years earlier with more mathematical and scientific fundamentals of chaos and systems theory, I felt still unhappy with the fact that I was aware that for some people in therapy and education this book might still be "too scientific".

As a consequence, I decided to work—additionally—on a second book which deals with the same core ideas and has the same message, but from different points of view and written in a rather "unscientific" way of writing. Without mentioning any formula or sharp terminology and in a more narrative stile, this book—entitled "Chaos, Fear and Order" (Engl. translation) —brings the idea of self-organization on different levels of human experience and interaction to the reader.

Both books were published at almost the same time, and some reviews referred to both of them. Although "Chaos, Fear and Order" has (until now) only two

editions, I am happy that it has prompted many more let-
ters than any other of my books. People I have never met
have before told me that they were challenged by the
ideas it contains.

The following chapter is based on the first chapter of
that book and is meant as an invitation to think about the
broader meaning of self-organization and actualization.

The Fear of Chaos

The sociologist Peter Berger has described a poignant
scene of the human struggle at the edges of chaos:

A child wakes up in the night, perhaps from a bad dream,
and finds himself surrounded by darkness, alone, beset by
nameless threats. At such a moment the contours of trusted
reality are blurred or invisible, and in the terror of incipient
chaos the child cries out for his mother. It is hardly an exag-
geration to say that, in this moment, the mother is being in-
voked as a high priestess of protective order. It is she (and, in
many cases, she alone) who has the power to banish the chaos
and to restore the benign shape of the world. And, of course,
any good mother will just do that. She will take the child and
cradle it in the timeless gesture of the Magna Mater... She will
speak or sing to the child, and the content of this communica-
tion will invariably be the same - „Don't be afraid - everything
is in order, everything is all right" If all goes well, the child
will be reassured, his trust in reality recovered, and in this
trust he will return to sleep. (Berger, 1970, p.61)

At numerous seminars and lectures I have experienced
how this description has really struck a chord deep within
the most disparate people. Without any lengthy introduc-
tions and explanations, this scene leads directly to the
heart of the conflict between chaos and order, a theme
which permeates every fiber of our existence. For every-

one can recall numerous similar scenes from his or her own life. And these are by no means limited to childhood experiences or to the consoling of children; chaos also lurks on the edges of existence for us so-called „healthy" adults. No matter how strong a bastion of safety, familiarity, routine and order we erect around us, cracks can unexpectedly appear in its facade. Dreams, extreme, unmanageable stress, blows of fate, or simply an inexplicable sensitivity can lead to shocks which cause a flood of thoughts and emotions to overwhelm us and can threaten to sweep our ordered lives into the abyss.

Indeed, a human being rarely feels more threatened than when the firm fabric of his existence begins to unravel—when all order collapses and he finds himself utterly exposed to the unexpected and unpredictable. Even relatively harmless signs of such an impending dissolution fill us with dread. In his "Existential Analysis of the Nature of Fear" the Viennese logotherapist and existential analyst Alfried Längle speaks of the human being's "basic fear". He describes this as the realization that "nothing is certain"—a realization involving such a shaking of life's sturdy foundation that stability and security appear to be seriously threatened (c.f. Längle 1996).

It is therefore most understandable when under certain circumstances a human being attempts to rally his last reserves to combat an imminent loss of stability and when, in his need—as numerous psychotherapeutical clinical case studies demonstrate—he attempts to extract a last remnant of order from the chaos enveloping him. Differing theories dealing with psychopathology do agree on one point—that many of the most clearly visible manifestations of human fear and mental illness have their origins in experienced chaos or in inappropriate attempts at banishing such chaos.

In numerous stories of creation and various myths, in fairy tales and legends dealing with the beginning and end of time, the threatening element of chaos appears again and again, a chaos whose etymological meaning is "unformed, shapeless primal cosmic mass, dissolution of all values, confusion." The Greek Hesoid (ca.700 B.C.) described chaos as the yawning, dark abyss which opened up between heaven and earth after the creation of the cosmos. And in an interpretation of Franz Josef Haydn's oratorio "The Creation" (1798) the author points out that chaos must first be overcome by life. "The instrumental introduction contains two basic motifs, a monotonous, gloomy tone and a cry echoing the struggle for life—chaos before the creation. In radiant C major to the sound of the full orchestra one hears the words 'Let there be light!' The first day of creation is dawning. The demons of the deep vanish."

There is, it is true, also the idea of chaos as a creative force — as described in many eastern philosophies or in the works of Paracelsus, Jacob Böhme, Georg C. Lichtenberg, Friedrich von Schlegel, Friedrich Nietzsche, Martin Heidegger and others, and most particularly in the works of the psychotherapists, from C. G. Jung to Carl Rogers and Fritz Perls and up to the systems and family therapists of today. However, all of these authors would appear to agree that the human being's tolerance of even such a positively interpreted chaos, that is chaos as a potential for creative change, is severely limited. In full force "the dissolution of all values and order" can at best only be endured as a relatively short transitional phase. Such a phase of radical change, in which all of the entrenched structures are thoroughly shaken must necessarily be followed by renewed order and a reduction of complexity. The regaining or retention of a certain stability and the familiar structures of our personal universe (Lebenswelt) is essential for our everyday lives.

The central question of this first chapter arises from the above experiences, descriptions and thoughts: just how do we so-called "normal" adults manage to banish fear-inducing chaos and to find meaning and order in this world? In contrast to children and many patients, for whom the introductory nightmare scene is a rather typical reflection of their personal universes, we seemingly take if for granted that we will live relatively undisturbed within our reality, the everyday reality of our society. Not only do others expect us to conform to this reality, we expect it of ourselves. And all this is in no way affected by the fact that our everyday reality displays tears and cracks about the edges. Indeed, we are fully justified in calling such phenomena merely peripheral areas of our normality. This question of just how we manage to banish chaos and to find meaning and order in this world has become increasingly topical in the last decades, for modern scientific research in the field of chaos and the systems theories has robbed us of our belief in an orderly world which for us is comprehensible, predictable and ultimately controllable. The image of our world as a gigantic clockwork which, when wound up, runs eternally according to some universal law of dynamics, was severely shaken at the turn of the century by quantum physics and the theory of relativity—and has since been utterly destroyed.

Instead, our modern view of the world again converges with the philosophies of various cultures and times (and with those of our own culture), in the awareness that the world is above all to be seen as an incredibly complex process, a process which we are intimately involved in and which we contribute to, but which for us, as part of the whole, must ultimately remain incomprehensible. Meaning and order can no longer be taken for granted. On the contrary, we are faced ever more often with the struggle to understand these concepts.

The concept of the world as a process alone exceeds human comprehension. For in a world which does not exist but merely occurs there is nothing substantial which can be relied upon eternally, which we can consider „eternal". On the contrary, everything is in a constant state of change. One cannot wade into the same river twice, as Heraclites long ago pointed out. As scientists we thus must recognize ever more clearly that our ordered systems are at best islands in a seething sea of chaos.

But if this thinking, with all its consequences, formed the structure of our personal universe we could not live in it. In a world in which we experienced solely the uniqueness of every moment and every space-time configuretion, in which therefore there were no recurring patterns, and as a result nothing familiar, paralyzing fear, such as one encounters in nightmares and psychotic illnesses, would be our constant companions. In such a world one could not physically survive, as we shall see later. It is therefore necessary to banish chaos and to provide our world with a certain order, regularity and reliability. It should be noticed that, in the field of clinical and so-called abnormal psychology we diagnose people as suffering from a lot categories of dis-"orders". But how is order achieved?

Avoiding Chaos by Means of Reduction

In order to continue the line of reasoning begun here it is important to understand that order for us is always the result of a reduction of complexity—an insight which is stressed not least of all in modern systems theories. We achieve this reduction by more or less chopping up the unique process of universal evolution—this chaos—into pieces, assigning these pieces to categories and thus inventing recurring patterns. By means of this creative dismembering the incomprehensible becomes, at least partially, comprehensible (for us).

I would like to illustrate this important point by means of the categories "evening" and "morning". We usually speak of these categories „evening" and „morning" as if they somehow actually existed—as if they were not our inventions but unquestionable constituents of reality. But strictly speaking, no evening in the history of the universe was exactly like the other and no morning identical to the other. And yet it is not only sensible to speak of evenings and mornings, it is essential for life that the sequence of these invented categories is seen as a rule. For only repetition makes both predictability and planning ahead possible, thus reducing our insecurity in dealing with our universe. We would not have been able to perform any of the acts or to take part in any of the activities which we experienced today if we had not created such recurring patterns.

It must be stressed that this reduction, i.e. categorical abstraction is by no means dependent on conceptualization and language—which limitation would mean that the creation of recurring patterns is primarily a human trait. On the contrary, this manner of gaining knowledge is apparently so basic and important for life in general that even its "lowest" forms have adapted evolutionarily to this (artificial and abstract) sequence of mornings and evenings. Where life forms have, for example, abstracted "light" from the endlessly complex process, the incomparability of mornings has been reduced to a single variable: "the reappearance of light"—and with regard to this one aspect all mornings are indeed the same.

In addition to this reduction involving "light" and thus the sequence and predictability of day and night, one also finds the construction of many more recurring patterns in evolution—low tide/high tide, spring/summer/fall/winter and many more, which are given labels such as "inborn triggering mechanisms", "instincts" and the like.

Life as we know it has, therefore, been wrested from chaos. It has established itself in an evolutionary process proceeding from the Big Bang as an alternative, so to speak, to the constantly recurring decay described in the field of thermodynamics. And all forms of life on this planet are dependent on the regularity, the recurring patterns that they create by means of reduction and abstraction. Friedrich Cramer, director for many years of the Max Planck Institute for experimental medicine in Göttingen, Germany, then uses the term "chaos avoidance strategies" in connection with life, from protein biosynthesis to complex biological processes, as well as to such cognitive inventions as art and aesthetics, and he stresses the fact that "order, development of life forms and creative power are the result of an inherent chaos avoidance, in the universe as in the life of each individual" (Cramer 1988).

Human Chaos Avoidance

Chaos avoidance is of particular importance for the human race, which has given its world an enormously complex system of rules, that which we refer to as "society" and "culture". Chaos, the infinite complexity of the unique world process, is apparently so threatening to us that evolutionary programs take effect virtually from the first day of our lives to wrest order from chaos and to seek out any possible „regularities" among the processes of the experienced world.

This becomes clear when one studies the innate abilities of babies. A new-born baby possesses, for example, the astonishing ability to break down the stream of sounds of any language spoken on this earth into its component parts. By means of single-frame analysis of filmed human communication one can demonstrate that when two adults converse they both produce slight movements, movements which the listener synchronizes with certain linguistic units (known as phonemes) uttered by the speaker. Babies only a few hours old are equally capable of moving synchronously in response to this linguistic structure, and this apparently, as stated above, in any existing language. What makes this particularly amazing is that we adults when listening to a truly foreign language with its foreign grammar cannot say where in the stream of sounds a particular word begins and ends. Such identification is necessary, of course, in order to learn any grammar, a system essentially based on the order of individual words. A new-born child, of course, also adjusts ever more to those sound patterns (words) which are used in the linguistic community it is living in. It can then distinguish these patterns ever more accurately and establishes a complex grammar, but in the process loses the ability to react to any other language.

In an even more impressive example the developmental psychologist Bower tells of a congenitally blind child which was given a radar-like position-finder with whose help every object within a radius of two meters was converted into audible frequencies, the pitch of the tone indicating the distance of an object and the volume its size. If an object moved towards the child the pitch and volume of the tone changed simultaneously. A few seconds after the installation of the device the baby knew that these changes indicated an object approaching its face. The salient point is that no baby had ever before been confronted with this type of specific information. Apparently the baby was able to utilize the equivalence of this acoustic information to that of the optical data and to react appropriately (see Bower 1978).

A different study of four-month-old infants showed that they were capable of detecting simple rules in the structure of their environments. That is, they were able to adapt quickly in reinforcement experiments involving the turning of their heads in certain patterns, such as "twice to the right", "three times to the right" and "right-left-change over." As only head movements of a certain extent were reinforced as correct "reactions", reactions failing to meet this criterion were not rewarded. This at first led to faulty "concepts", until by "testing" various "hypotheses" the babies arrived at the correct strategy.

All three of the studies used as examples here demonstrate that the search for possible regularities in the environment is also an inborn trait of human beings, and that rules and order are apparently of central importance. Even in those cases in which the search for rules should actually fail—because psychologists in laboratory experiments have so created a segment of the world that it is sure to contain n o order—structured order is established. This is demonstrated by, among others, an old experiment dealing with the psychology of perception. On a board containing, say, ten rows of ten lightbulbs, each bulb is connected to a random generator and therefore lights up at irregular intervals. The observer, however, by no means sees lights flashing on at random—what he sees instead is moving structured shapes (or so-called "Gestalten").

Gestalt psychology, a theoretically and experimentally significant branch of psychology during the first decades of this century (until its disbanding by the Nazi regime), worked out how actively organized our knowledge of the world is even on the lowest sensory level. Sensory perception is to be regarded as a complex process, in which stimuli are converted into "Gestalten"—a process which is described in, among others, so-called "Gestalt" laws. We automatically organize dots on a piece of paper to patterns and pictures and perceive a sequence of tones, if at all possible, as a "melody", the elements within these arrangements (dots or tones) often receiving new and specific meaning—for example this gives rise to the phenomenon known as the "leading tone" of a melody. Such findings exist in numerous variations—also involving the creation of more complexly structured order. Moving geometric figures, for example, can thus, under certain circumstances, produce a vivid impression of typical "social interactions" or "causes and effects". This, too, has been the subject of numerous psychological experiments. In principle, however, we have already encountered this phenomenon in animated films—where it is then particularly impressive when the moving shapes do not possess human or animal forms at all, in fact do not have any similarity to them, but rather any other forms whatever. Even then the way the shapes coordinate their movements and approach one another still creates the overwhelming impression that here one is dealing with "living creatures" or even "human beings" who are interacting.

This fundamentally constructive nature of at least parts of our "Erfahrungswelt" (experienced world) can hardly be demonstrated more clearly. We cannot and need not go into detail here, but the examples show that beginning at a very elementary level of perception, even before our consciousness intervenes with deliberate decisions, our impressions are always experienced as parts of a structured world. And in the process of establishing order, of banishing chaos, we invent rules and regularity as the need arises.

This active search for regularities and the organization of stimuli it involves also applies in a similar form to practically all "life rules" (without explaining this more fully here). Some of the principles of organization have been acquired in the course of evolution—as, for example, figure-background differentiation and other aspects of Gestalt perception. And in other areas as well the inborn contribution should not be underestimated: speech, sexual behavior, social relations, panic reactions, logical thought processes and the like are influenced to a substantial degree by the structuring principles which have emerged during the process of evolution.

However, for human beings it is significant that they can go beyond these evolutionarily and biologically acquired rules to adapt them individually and socially, and even to invent entirely new areas of rules. These are particularly useful in the individual's adaptation to his or her personal living conditions (in a more narrow sense).

Between Chaos and Order

Establishing order is therefore extremely necessary. For it wards off the unfathomable distress that we would otherwise fall prey to in our experiential chaos—a chaos in comparison with which the above-mentioned psychotic breakdowns and nightmares would seem to be no more than harmless preliminary stages. For this reason we should appreciate this positive aspect of order. The reduction of a complex, unique process to recurring classes of phenomena gives structure to chaos, makes predictions possible and reduces insecurity, thus creating reliability. And this reliable order is with us from the first days of our life.

Let us recall the scene involving the mother who banishes chaos for her child by being, as Berger puts it, a high priestess of order. She sings, we are told, a lullaby.

Now, songs are the embodiment of regularity; lullabies and evening songs in particular possess simple, repeated sequences of tones, for they sing of the rising moon, the starry sky, the approaching dawn—phenomena which are recurrent and predictable. And, above all, these songs and their words can be repeated again and again in the same manner. We all know the reaction of many small children: "Oh, can't you sing me ... again?" And preferably it is those songs which they have already heard a thousand times or more. And woe unto you if you make any changes! What is needed to soothe a child is not something new but rather that which occurs again and again.

The fact that, strictly speaking, the singing of every song is a world premiere—unique, at no time before or after existing in exactly this form, just like every evening and every morning, just like everything we experience— this particular aspect plays no role at all. In contrast, we abstract that which the phenomena have in common, that which is similar, or in other words, familiar. Everything then is so safe, so familiar, that one no longer needs to listen and to pay attention carefully and can, like the child, doze off.

But he who now mentally slips into an idyllic imaginary world where all is familiar, so familiar that he need no longer listen carefully—he has forgotten to take the needs of his spouse or companion into account:

"Really! You aren't listening to me!" or "You aren't really listening to me!" Who is not familiar with such reproachful exclamations?

And here we see the other side of the chaos coin. We have, it is true, just stressed, in a kind of provisional conclusion, that the reduction of a complex, unique process to recurring classes of phenomena gives chaos structure, reduces uncertainty, makes predictability and reliability possible and creates, as it were, familiarity. But now we must add that this reduction to that which is all too familiar limits the ability to grasp uniqueness and closes our eyes to the creative side of the life process.

In contrast to the situation in which a lullaby is sung and a soothing familiarity is conjured up, there are many situations in which our spouses, companions and others have a strong interest in their words being given the status of a „world premiere", in our really getting involved in what they have to say which is new and unique, or simply in their manner of relating to us here and now. And if we become involved at least somewhat in this uniqueness something like a personal encounter could take place.

If, however, we merely glean that which is known and familiar to us from the words and situation, and then respond with, to ourselves or out loud, „Oh, I already know that!", if we already tune out after the third word, pursuing our own thoughts and not listening to what is new, then what takes place will not be a personal encounter but merely an exchange of empty phrases, an acting out of tired rituals. And then trouble is often unavoidable. For our partner then feels, rightfully so, that he or she is not being perceived as a person but misused as an easily replaceable object whose only purpose is to set our own schemata (i.e. cognitive patterns) in motion. Even on the level of technical discussions, in which a personal exchange is not necessarily desirous, we are expected to be receptive to the new information and not to always act as if we already knew how each sentence would end and what the other had to say.

The fact that everyone is only too familiar with such situations, however, shows the effectiveness of a mechanism which primarily causes us to comb our experienced world in search of recurring patterns. Indeed, the same process which creates order and security—namely the reduction to familiar categories—is at the same time the kiss of death for creativity and change. And this is where unnecessary, compulsive order can set in. By means of illustration I would like to use an example that again commences with evenings and mornings:

When someone says "I got up at seven o'clock every morning this week, had breakfast with my wife", etc., he is not just sticking to society's division of time into "days" and „hours" (using an unbiological precision or "punctuality"). On the contrary, he is failing to mention that the spectacular rosy dawn in the clear, cold air last Tuesday "morning" was completely different from the incomparable scene of a fog-shrouded "morning" sun on Wednesday, and that this in turn was something totally different from the sparkling world of glittering raindrops on Thursday "morning" (to name only a few possible aspects of "mornings").

In this example I am not interested in phenomena of language. We need such linguistic reductions, above all in everyday life. They are undoubtedly important in helping us to communicate quickly. No, here I am interested in the question of whether anything more than just a stereotyped category, "mornings", was "perceived" and "experienced", or whether at least—under less stress—something more than and different from such "mornings" can be experienced—and moreover, whether it was noticed at all that actually—despite being the product of human planning—"the breakfast" also displayed many differing details "every morning" and always tasted different. This last point is true not only because no two breadrolls are identical but rather because we cannot and should not ever feel exactly the same about anything if we are still capable of clearly experiencing our own life reality. And because our perceptions and their cognitive processing are strongly influenced by our moods and emotions, even two identical breadrolls will, depending on our mood, taste different.

When, however, that which we experience out of the possible variety and complexity is reduced to categories such as "had breakfast" at "every morning" we should then not be surprised if "every evening" "the same arguments" about "the same problems" always crop up. For the same reduction to (too) few and (too) rigid categories also takes effect in the structuring of our social sphere. In our interactions with spouses, children and others it is again just "the same old story". Therapists encounter this excessive reduction, this experiential impoverishment in many of the people who sit across from them. But who among us can claim that he himself does not react similarly, at least to a degree, or even possibly much too strongly and much too often?

Seen from this angle the ways of encountering the "world" can be placed on a scale between two diametrically opposed poles.

At the one extreme end we find the chaotic, the unpredictable, and the highly complex. And the more we become involved with the uniqueness of processes the less reduced are our experiences, which now are more likely to admit the awareness of the new, the surprising and the creative. But therefore we are less able to create categories, cannot make predictions based on regularities and are all the more likely to fall prey to the fear of the unpredictable and uncontrollable.

At the other extreme end we find reductive order. And the more we categorize at this other end and detect or invent recurring aspects and regularities, the more predictable and therefore safer our experience of the world becomes. As a result chaos is held in check or even banished. But we find the "things" treated in this manner all the more rigid, boring, reduced and uniform.

The Social Banishing of Chaos

A human being does not, of course, find his particular position in the area of conflict between these two poles all by himself. On the contrary, a prospective member of our culture is born into a stable system composed of social interaction, established institutions and material structures. Long before we walk out onto life's stage the scenery in this never-ending drama has been put in place and our roles at least roughly prescribed by bundles of expectations. And our very first steps on this stage are accompanied by—if not actually controlled by—instructions governing actions and meaning which are intended, as systems of rules, to reduce complexity and banish chaos. For example, two significant systems of rules are the oral and written forms of language. In addition, our culture in particular has created regularity by processing materials into commodities (in the broadest sense of the term). We need only look around us: there is hardly anything unspoiled and natural to be seen, hardly anything that has not been processed or adapted to different uses or even created wholly by man. Tools, vehicles, buildings, clothing, works of art (in the broadest sense) devices used for mass communication, etc.—all have a strong influence on our sensorial impressions.

The experiences which are possible with these objects are by no means chaotic but rather highly regulated and ordered. At the very latest the socialization process sees to this, that is to say, the education we receive from school, the workplace and all the other social institutions. A fork is not to be used for scratching but must be employed in a prescribed manner if one is to avoid the embarrassment of bad manners and the subsequent tutoring in deportment this would entail. It is just the same with a fountain pen, which is not meant to be thrown about or used to spear pieces of food—indeed, in school it is not even to be used for "scrawling about" but is reserved for certain highly regulated movements which result in the production of highly standardized symbols. Usually the creativity which is invested in inventing such objects serves to limit creativity in the use of the objects and to establish regularity.

Such routine behavior does, of course, provide the freedom one needs to be creative in other areas. Thus the correct, rule-conforming use of a fountain pen, a type-writer or a computer saves a lot of time and energy (compared to the quill or the chisel used in cuneiform writing), which one could use, for example, for the development and recording of original ideas—perhaps in the form of a poem or a scientific treatise. But before we overrate the freedom to be creative gained as a result of rules one should ask oneself just how many of all the people who use a fountain pen, a typewriter or a computer are really able or allowed to use these apparatus to creatively express their inner selves. Most people probably use these apparatus within a framework of activities in which they are not self-determined but rather subjected to rules and constraints.

Next to meaningfully transformed matter regularly structured social relations are the second large sphere in which the human being establishes a world with an order he has wrested from chaos. Our modern societies in particular are distinguished by the fact that ever more areas which were formerly reserved for the spontaneous activities and initiative of the individual have now been systematically regimented by means of compulsory rules. There has been a steady increase not only in the number of laws and ordinances and the wide range of areas they regulate, but also in the spectrum of duties organizations and institutions perform.

People who do not fit within this system of rules and who are likely to spread chaos—the mentally retarded and ill, the physically handicapped, the homeless and others—are shunted aside and handed over to the appropriate institutions. Starting with infant care and kindergarten and progressing to mental hospitals and homes of every kind for the mentally retarded, and finally to special wards in hospitals where the dying are cared for professionally, the chaos in and caused by these human beings is banished to the periphery of our normal, everyday life. These areas of life go largely unnoticed in our "usual" daily routine and are, accordingly, also as strictly regulated as is conceivably possible. But the persons in care, if not others as well, do not perceive this tendency to regulate life as a positive, creative order but rather as isolation and subjugation involving an imposed order.

A young human being is exposed to strict regulation in a similar fashion. As a result, his highly complex and often bewildering, unpredictable reactions are—as Heinz v. Foerster puts it —"trivialized": young Fritz is in school and perhaps his answer to the question "How much is three times three?" is: "green!". But this creative answer is, of course, not permissible. Therefore he is taught that to answer the question "How much is three times three?" reliably, predictably and reproducibly he must say "nine!" (c.f. v.Foerster 1988). However, it must be said that, for example, in the course of formal education—or the socialization process in general—knowledge and behavior are differentiated. But these differentiations take place within the narrow framework of society's approved system of rules. And the fact that it is western civilization which has shown a particularly strong tendency to reduction and to order based on control has been of much consequence. For this culture is more likely to tempt us to banish chaos not only by necessary means but to approach too avidly the order end of the scale and to thereby establish more restraints than are needed. This is closely connected with the dominant concepts of order.

On "Law and Order"

In our society the term „order" is often closely connected to the idea of „putting something in order", that is, establishing orderliness. We need only think of the areas we live and work in—desk, kitchen, and apartment. We must intervene daily to transform the seemingly self-generating untidiness into orderliness.

Isn't this what we experience every day in other areas of our lives? And don't we hear, from the leading politicians of our state and from many who elect them, the call for "law and order"?—which as a rule is synonymous with the call for forces whose task it is to prevent chaos from developing or spreading: clear laws, specific institutions and rules, and police and other law—enforcement agencies which can impose order from without and if need be preserve it by constantly intervening. For roughly 300 years this view has been held and supported by western science. Indeed, one can even call this view an essential guiding principle in the development of this science, as will be elaborated on later in chapter three. Further back in time, in the Middle Ages the acknowledged goal of science was rather to understand nature in order to act in harmony with it. But in the 17th century, with the development of the experimental method and mathematical analysis, together with the application of the newly-gained knowledge to expand technology, scientific research received a new image and goal: It was now a matter of subjugating nature and dominating, controlling, and ruling it.

And are not indeed the achievements of technology clear proof that the world can be reshaped and ruled? Engines, automobiles, airplanes, the chemistry of synthetics and the biochemistry of medical technology, our advances in the microscopic world with nuclear fission and atomic power and in outer space with the moon landings and space probes—doesn't all this show the triumph of the human mind over nature?

If one follows the media and the press releases of the politicians, it all too often appears as if one must answer this question in the affirmative. But today more and more people realize that despite all its progress, classical western science has also created a tremendous potential for destruction. It didn't take Chernobyl and uranium smuggling to teach us that the security of nuclear reactors and weapons cannot be guaranteed.

The eradication of diseases such as tuberculosis, cholera and typhoid has not provided us with absolute control over disease, as the rapid increase in the incidence of cancer, heart disease and AIDS shows clearly. Our airplanes have undoubtedly become safer and in the area of industrial production we have mastered numerous complicated manufacturing technologies. But we have paid for this with a depleted ozone layer, acid raid and numerous other environmental problems.

Today science itself has also had to radically revise its view of life. Modern chaos research and systems theories of the last two or three decades have, as stated earlier on, destroyed once and for all the long-held belief in the fundamental calculability of "the world". Consequently, the concepts regarding order also had to be revised—at least in academic circles. Though it is not possible to elaborate on chaos research here, one of the key findings is that unspecific ambient conditions of a system are enough in themselves to enable it to unfold its own internal order. This means that these structures of order are present as possibilities within the system. And although they are encouraged and, after a fashion, caused to unfold by external conditions, the resulting order as such is not introduced from without.

These phenomena are downright typical of all manner of life processes. This became clear when scientists began to see their world through different eyes and suddenly discovered self-organizing processes everywhere. From a biological-medical standpoint the organization and function of organs such as heart, kidneys, lungs, lymph glands, central nervous system and others have been described very accurately by means of chaos- and self-organization theories. The same is true of psychic and communication processes.

Thereby natural science has at last begun to deal with something which has always been available to the vast majority of human beings as alternative knowledge. A mother who carries her child under her heart, a farmer or a gardener—they have always been confronted daily with the knowledge that the complex order which they see developing around them can by no means be considered solely the result of their personal power and control over things. Such people have always interpreted "law and order", the favorite slogan of conservative politicians, differently: namely, that only through trust in the "laws" of nature and through the greatest possible harmony with them can one support those processes which call forth an autonomous order or enable an inherent order to develop. From this life-oriented point of view an entirely different conception of order can be seen: here one must trust rather than do or control. One can only support that which is already present or arranged, as order emerges on its own—under conditions, to be sure, that one can influence. This last aspect is dealt with more thoroughly within the framework of the so-called self-organization theories.

When we think of the mother and her unborn child, growth processes in nature, the development of personal gifts and the question of what we must do to make our partner love us we should not find it difficult to recognize the absurdity of control-ideology. Even the mother in the opening anecdote was not primarily conveying to her child: "I have got everything under control", but rather: "Everything is all right", in the sense of: "Have trust in being and becoming".

And still we experience again and again how difficult it is for us to have such trust—even when we are reasonable enough to recognize that control would also not be of any help to us. As parents involved in the upbringing and education of our children, as therapists accompanying patients during transitional phases, and in many similar situations, we often feel incapable of mustering the trust needed to avoid intervening too much from the side of order, limiting ourselves instead to merely providing improved and helpful conditions. We give in all too easily to the powerful "law and order" ideology.

How Relationships Become Rigid

Therapists often observe in the dynamics of families and couples that banishing chaos by means of order can easily destroy an adequate equilibrium between uniqueness and regularity. Then, the human beings become the victim of a self-inflicted compulsory order. This is because the family, as part of the general social framework, plays a special role with regard to the creation of order. This results from the high level of intimacy and physical contact between members of a family as well as the security and confirmation of personal worth they expect from their interactions. In addition, communication for the most part is face to face, which is to say that what one person expresses is to a very large degree the impression the other person receives and vice versa—interactions with immediate feedback.

At the same time, however, these familial interactions must always pass through each family member's personal "bottle-neck" of interpretation. And now the mechanism described above in its effects on the individual can become fully effective—or even fully destructive. When our total possible experience of the world is reduced too strongly by schemata and we address ourselves less to that which is unique and more to that which seems to us to be always the same, our personal relationships will soon indeed be characterized by the repetition of rigid behavior patterns.

Therapists who deal with families and couples often observe how reactions to another person's forms of expressing himself have less to do with the communication itself than with some curious rules: off-hand one could say that the attempt at communication made by one person—let's call her Ute—as registered and processed by the other person—let's call him Peter—merely acts as a general trigger which causes an "inner film" of expected meaning to start to play. So, as I explained earlier, Peter does not actually listen any more. In certain situations if Ute merely opens her mouth he already knows "what's up". At least he thinks he knows. But how can he know for sure if he doesn't really listen any more? At any rate, what Peter is reacting to is more his "inner film" than what Ute has said. For therapists the following brief exchange is therefore typical:

Therapist: What did you perceive?

Peter: The way Ute looked at me I knew what to expect.

Therapist: Did you hear what she said?

Peter: No, I already know what she is going to say when she looks at me like that.

When Ute becomes aware that Peter's reactions to much of what she says are always the same because he doesn't listen, she will go to less effort to come up with anything new. This in turn confirms Peter in his belief that he was right in thinking that "Ute always goes on about the same old things." Unfortunately, it is not only Peter who is affected in this manner. We could have observed and related this whole interaction from Ute's point of view. Here a vicious circle of reduction has been set in motion in which both partners appear to be both active participants and victims of circumstance at the same time. Sadly, this commingling of the roles of perpetrator and victim is typical of many social relationships.

Those interpretation patterns and forms of behavior which (in the sense of the interpretations) are mutually confirmable develop especially well during the common development of a family or a couple. Hence, these persons' degree of freedom can under unfavorable circumstances become increasingly restricted. This results in a situation which an observer experiences and describes as "encrusted, rigid structures". The wife's most likely different utterances and their intentions are all reduced to the category of "nagging", and this is what her husband reacts to. There are simply far too few categories at hand that could be used to understand the partner's behavior.

When families submit themselves to therapy their therapists do actually find that in the course of time the spectrum of possible behavior patterns (and how these were perceived and mentally interpreted) has been reduced to a few different categories. The degree to which the "overly familiar" has insinuated itself, as it does into every family in time, has increased enormously. The family member does not react to what was said but to what (in his own personal conviction) this means and what the other person is imputed to have really said.

As a result such a family system is also often incapable of utilizing spontaneous creativity in a member's behavior to effect change—for such creative behavior is effectively neutralized by the interpretation categories.

Furthermore, these assumptions which are significant for actions are not tested for their veracity because as self-fulfilling prophecies they are constantly being confirmed by (reduced) perception. Because this process is to a large degree an unconscious one and one cannot (meta)-communicate about it, a family at this stage is caught in its own web of actions, perceptions and mental interpretations. May be by this point the family needs outside help.

This outline was intended to make clear how our essential ability to reduce chaos and complexity to categories can, under unfavorable conditions, turn into self-reinforcing, rigid patterns of cognitive and interactive processes in which one is trapped as a victim while at the same time participating in the interactions as a perpetrator. A society obsessed with an ideology based on power and order can paralyze the creativity in the lives of the individuals as well as in those of partners, couples, friends, families, and other social institutions. Then, our encounters with the world, with other people, and ultimately with ourselves, become rigid and governed by abstract categories—sometimes far from real needs, real feelings, real meanings and, at worst, far from reality at all.

On Incongruence

In the person-centered approach of Carl Rogers, it is known that it is not only (self-)actualization, but also incongruence that plays a central role. "Incongruence" means the lack of adequate conceptualizations or "symbolizations" of organic (sensory and visceral) experiences. According to a proposition of Rogers' theory of personality, not all values and evaluations are adequate descriptions of one's experience. In contrast, during the course of a child's development, social evaluations by others become part of the phenomenal field not as experiences that involve other but rather as introjections— for example "this behavior of mine is bad", where the correct symbolization "I experience that my parents experience this behavior to be unsatisfying to them" is distorted into "I perceive this behavior to be unsatisfying".

Similarly, the expression of anger comes to be "experienced" as bad, even though the more accurate symbolization would be that the expression of anger is often experienced as satisfying. Thus, Rogers stresses "The values attached to experiences ... in some instances are values introjected or taken over from others, but perceived in distorted fashion, as if they had been experienced directly" (Rogers 1951, p. 498). Consequently, in a later proposition, the benefit of person-centered psychotherapy is described by the following: "As the individual perceives and accepts into his self-structure more of his organic experience, he finds that he is replacing his present value system—based so largely upon introjections which have been distorted symbolized—with a continuing organismic valuing process" (ibid. 522).

Focused on the congruence and incongruence of experience and its symbolization, Rogers seem to discuss the same challenge of the tension between unique, complex, unspeakable and indescribable processes of experience and the necessity of nevertheless referring, understanding, symbolizing, and communicating these experiences by way of language and its categories, which entail abstraction and reduction.

This becomes even more clear in a statement by Rogers in the context of interpersonal relationship (Rogers 1961, p 341): "There is an important corollary of the construct of congruence which is not at all obvious. It may stated in this way. If an individual is at the moment entirely congruent, his actual physiological experience being accurately represented in his awareness, then his communication could never contain an expression of an external fact. If he was congruent he could not say, 'That rock is hard'; 'He is stupid'; 'You are bad'; or 'She is intelligent.' The reason for this is that we never experience such 'facts'. Accurate awareness of experience would always be expressed as feelings, perceptions, and meanings from an inner frame of reference. I never know that he is stupid or you are bad. I can only perceive that you seem this way to me. Likewise, strictly speaking I do not know that the rock is hard, even though I may be very sure that I experience it as hard if I fall down on it. (And even then I can permit the physicists to perceive it as a very permeable mass of high-speed-atoms and molecules.) If the person is thoroughly congruent then it is clear that all of his communication would necessarily be put in a context of personal perception."

The discussion of (in)congruence deals with the question of how much an experience is adequately (or, due to introjections, distorted) symbolized by this process of abstraction and reduction. Our discussion focused the problem onto abstraction and reduction in a broader sense—making clear that, on the one hand, even human "experience" is reduced and pre-structured by evolution and that, on the other hand, the process of symbolizing is embedded in social structures and their interconnectedness with categories, meaning-structures, metaphors, and narratives. Moreover, these social structures influence and are influenced by processes on different levels—an encounter between two people, family interactions, processes in organizations and in society as a whole (to mention only some levels and areas).

Of course, many therapists, counselors, educators and others share the message that the more we become involved with the uniqueness of here-and-now processes, the less reduced our experiences are by symbolization, which are then more likely to admit the awareness of the new, the surprising and the creative. But if we move too far onto to the side of chaos—to the unpredictable and complex—the price is that we cannot make predictions based on regularities and are all the more likely to fall prey to the fear of the unpredictable and uncontrollable.

However, extreme reductive order, established from outside by way of introjections or values and prescriptions which turn out to be more or less inadequate for the processes of life, doesn't seem not to be the right solution. The more we categorize and detect or invent recurring aspects and regularities, the more predictable and therefore safer our experience of the world becomes. As a result, chaos is held in check or even banished. But we find the "things" treated in this manner all the more rigid, boring, reduced and uniform. The necessary order has to be adaptive to conditions, constraints and requirements on different levels, in different situations and to different needs and values. Therefore order can not simply be prefabricated, but also has to combine the aspects of both security and creativity. Actualization of self-organized order—in other words: Trust in being and becoming—is the general message shared by wise old sayings in various cultures, Humanistic Psychology, and Therapy and modern systems theory.

The following chapters will discuss this in more detail.

References

Berger, P.L. (1970). A Rumor of Angels. Modern Society and the Rediscovery of the Supernatural. New York: Doubleday

Bower, T. (1978). Die Wahrnehmungswelt des Kindes. Stuttgart: Klett-Cotta

Cramer, F. (1988). Chaos und Ordnung. Die komplexe Struktur des Lebendigen. Stuttgart: DVA

Foerster, H.v. (1988). Abbau und Aufbau. In:Simon, F. (Hrsg.): Lebende Systeme. Berlin: Springer, 19-33

Längle, A. (1996). Der Mensch auf der Suche nach Halt. Existenzanalyse der Angst. Bull.d.Ges.f. Logotherapie und Existenzanalyse, 13,2,4-12

Rogers, C.R. (1951). The Client-centered therapy; its current practice, implications, and theory. Boston: Houghton

Rogers, C.R.(1961). On Becoming a Person. A therapist's view of psychotherapy. London: Constable

Chapter 3

OUR 'LEBENSWELT' IN UPHEAVAL

In the spring and summer of 2003 the University of Vienna bestowed upon me the "Paul-Lazarsfeld-Gast-professur". This guest professorship was founded in 2001 in honor of Paul F. Lazarsfeld (*1901 Vienna, +1976 New York), a famous scientist in the fields of psychology and social sciences—and particularly well known for his contributions to research methodology. Paul Lazarsfeld worked at the University of Vienna until 1935, when he fled the NAZI-Regime and went into exile in the United States, where he worked at Princeton and Columbia. After WWII, Lazarsfeld used his influential positions (p.e. at the Rockefeller Foundation and Ford Foundation) to help Austrian's scientific institutions in their post-war rebuilding. He was one of the founders of the "Institute for Advanced Studies" in Vienna (where I worked as a young student from '66-'70).

Besides my regular teaching in psychotherapy and clinical psychology as well as research methods at the psychological department and, in addition, a dozen lectures at different departments, I was invited to give a lecture in the town hall of Vienna to an even broader audience. They asked me to bring together, if possible, psychological, sociological and historical aspects.

While working on this theme, I became more and more fascinated by the interconnectedness of historical, social, familial and personal aspects – an interconnection that I had overlooked before. I became aware of interwoven processes that are normally divided and addressed by different areas or levels of investigation.

This chapter is a translation of the core sections of a small book which was published (as part of a series of selected Vienna town-hall lectures) on the basis of this lecture. I was trying to bring to an heterogeneous audience the idea of how individual experience and its congruent and incongruent processes of symbolization—and the expression and (self-)understanding of psychopathological symptoms—are embedded in the processes of familial narratives which, again, are embedded in the processes of narratives of society as a whole. And that, of course, these cognitive and interactive processes are related to biographical and historical "facts"—which, especially in the Europe of the 20th century, were very often literally "unspeakable".

Interwoven Micro and Macro Processes

The German word Lebenswelt refers to our personal experience and understanding of the world, including the individual, social, political, and environmental perspectives. These structures function in our everyday experience without becoming explicitly conscious or even an object of reflection. One's Lebenswelt is experienced and anticipated as coherent, consistent, and meaningful. It is, however, informed by 'data' (knowledge and information) from scientists, politicians, mass media and others who purport to provide an objective perspective of the world. This 'data' is idealized and abstracted from the personal Lebenswelt by means of explicit reflection, including particular techniques of observation.

When we speak of upheaval in our world, it probably first brings to mind macroscopic social and environmenttal structures. According to surveys and analyses in the media, it seems that people are indeed feeling some serious concern in response to major disruptions in these areas.

* The so-called iron curtain has disappeared, only to reveal other political hot spots around the globe. In the aftermath of our focus on East-West problems, what have emerged into the foreground are the discrepancies between the first and third worlds and a growing tension between religious communities.

* The events of September 11th, 2001 (exactly 28 years after the Pinochet coup and the death of Allende in Chile on September 11th 1973) have called for radical changes in our security systems. In spite of—or more accurately because of—our highly developed technology and our trust in the efficacy of our security systems in the first world, these structures have become vulnerable and can now be penetrated by fanatics armed with nothing more than a box knife. The question arises of whether tighter control measures and improved technology are really appropriate steps towards providing long-term security in our culture? Perhaps what is called for is a sober examination of the reasons behind the problems and a look at some methods for dealing with those issues. In view of the increase in poverty for an ever-larger segment of the population, we also need to ask whether protecting the growing wealth of our culture is even a viable option.

* There are signs of upheaval in all those systems in which stability is overly dependent upon an economic model of growth. It has become increasingly clear that our systems of health, retirement, and education, as straightforward as they once seemed, are no longer affordable. At the same time, there are no alternatives being developed to economically based growth, and there do not appear to be any convincing visions of a functioning society without such economic growth. In the media we can watch an army of specialists, with a wide range of short-term solutions, all being helplessly driven by the political forces of the day.

The effects of these macroscopic changes, together with our shaken sense of security, prompt most of us to ask where this is all leading. At the same time there is an underlying echo at the personal level that asks, "Where is this all leading for me and for my family?" This is an illustration of the interwoven nature of micro and macro perspectives that seems to be typical of the structure of our Lebenswelt. The immediate reference points are those aspects of life and surroundings that relate to the individual—more specifically, to me and the effects on me at the center of my own personal Lebenswelt, but also accompanied by a sense of the individual firmly embedded within the social processes of society.

I would like to look at these general connections using a vignette from a session that took place only a few days ago. As I was preparing the material for this speech, I was, of course, especially attuned to these particular issues.

For some years we have offered a clinical seminar at the university, in cooperation with a large psychiatric clinic. The students who attend are nearing the end of their course of study and have already had some therapeutic training. For each seminar, an inpatient from the clinic is invited to participate in a two-hour session.

The program is highly regarded, not only by the students, but also by the patients and the therapists from the clinic who are present for the sessions. Everyone clearly reaps some benefit.

The first part of the session consists of an interview detailing the family case history, usually conducted by my colleague or me individually, (or together, whenever that is possible). Names and dates are collected of siblings, parents, grandparents, and so on, and including spouses and children whenever applicable. In addition to birth dates, patients are asked to report marriages, divorces, any important job-related events, or other relevant aspects of life. All this information is presented on a large board as a so-called family genogram. These simple, factual bits of information often combine to provide an impressive picture of various connections in the patient's history, and there may be some particular aspects that stand out. For example, there might be a first name that runs through several generations, perhaps even the patient's name. It may be obvious that there is a lot of information about the father's family, but almost none regarding that of the mother. Connections between deaths or births and particular crises become clear. Comments (and laments) typical in this family often come out with no prompting, and may reflect an amazing congruence or contradiction with one another, or with the issues that are important to this patient.

In terms of macro and micro systems, we could say that a basic overview emerges of the disruptions and upheavals that have had particular meaning in the history of the individual members of the multi-generational family, but also in relation to the family fate as a whole. In the context of 20th century European history, these events are usually related to historical changes and disruptions such as expulsion, re-location, deportation or emigration, long periods of imprisonment, and war-related deaths of young mothers or fathers. The bare facts and dates allow a brief but penetrating look into complex, difficult fates.

One can easily assume that there is even more fragmentation that has been painstakingly patched, scarred over, and covered up in connection with historical maelstroms such as the Nazi dictatorship and the entanglements of that guilt.

Without a lot of discussion or explanation, it becomes clear how upheaval and change have called up the family's creative resources, and often may have led to rather unconventional solutions to problems. We might notice indications of a relationship between those emergency solutions and the present suffering. In addition, we might also get a glimpse of what is now preventing the usual dynamics of everyday life from initiating change—the kind of disruption that might interrupt this daily repetition of incapacitating symptoms and introduce a transition from patterns seen as dysfunctional to patterns that are experienced as healthy.

In summary, the task is to look at the way in which symptoms may be embedded within a meaningful network. The central question is not one of causes or blame (a point of reference that is prevalent, and usually obstructive in our daily life), but rather a question of what these symptoms are stabilizing and what is standing in the way of change. I will return to this issue later.

The orientation of the interview focuses attention on the significance of the social system called 'family' even though normally only the patient is present, and not the whole family. Some may find this focus surprising in view of how much we hear these days about the waning influence of the family. Statistics document startling increases in divorces, singles, patchwork families, single parents, and so on, which imply significant changes in our concept and experience of family in today's society. It is clear that everyday reality no longer corresponds to the ad industry's image of the 'average family': mother, father, two children, a dog, happy smiling faces, and lots of time for each other. You can be sure, however, that these out-dated images are not due to any ignorance on the part of the ad industry; the image creators are well aware of the changes that have taken place. In contrast to the social-demographic changes, there is still a strong undercurrent in our culture that carries longings that are connected to, and stimulated by, those images.

More importantly in terms of our discussion, the family is always present as a mediator between the micro and macro processes that determine the essence of our culture. In this sense, it is irrelevant whether the family is a patchwork or fragmented family. Long before the school and other formal institutions have a chance to intervene, children relate to the social community through their families. Our family anchors us in our own history and the history of previous generations. The determinates of a particular culture are taken for granted within the family — the rules and taboos, the degree of freedom that is permissible, and a determination of what is meaningful and what is not. The family is also the foundation for the development of individuality, but an individuality that always co-develops within the context of the family.

Herein lies the double message "be one of us," and simultaneously, "be who you are," a dialectical contradiction that challenges a developing young person to the utmost.[1] In addition to providing a pattern for social relationships, the family is also a surface for the projection of wishes, needs, and fantasies in regards to security, trust and intimacy.

What the images of advertising dangle before our eyes is a fulfillment of these basic needs. Regardless of what

---

[1] It should be noted that 'be' is not meant statically, but dynamically. Stemming from the Sanskrit word 'bhu' (=growing) it has much more the meaning of 'becoming'

the empirical analyses of social science report about the objective state of today's families, the cognitive-imaginative system 'family'—a multi-generational entity—continues to be the implicit and explicit frame of reference for structuring the connections between the individual's life and the culture.

The basic structures of what we call 'reality' are developed in early childhood in the context of cognitive social patterns and the associated narratives we tell ourselves about them. Therefore, a consideration of these specific structures is informative for everyone.

The case I would like to use as an example involves a woman in her mid-thirties, who was suffering from compulsive disorder;[2] the details of her compulsions are not significant here. Both of her parents came from families in which there had been three major disruptive events. Her grandparents on her father's side came from what is now Russia, and her maternal grandparents came from what is now Poland. In addition to the war and the collapse of value systems in response to Third Reich propaganda, both families had also been driven from their homes. A third serious disruption in each of the families was that the parents had separated when their children (the patient's mother and father) were young.

The patient's mother and father had remained together in their marriage but, I would say, at the price of a certain degree of hardening and rigidity. Her father was described as a very crusty, authoritarian man who placed an extremely high value on order. He had never developed a compulsive disturbance, but he had chosen a profession

---

[2] Typically, the English word 'dis-order' implies the tacit ideology that illness of the psyche has to do with a lack of order, and that health is related to order. On a socio-political level, the justification for military intervention is in order (!) to impose order through force. In contrast, the perspective in this article is that in cases of neurosis we find a sense of order that is excessive, over-simplified, and rigidified.

in which the orderly organization of facts and figures was a central aspect. The patient's mother was portrayed as a woman who conformed completely to this life style. The central leitmotifs in this patient's life were "I always have to be strong" and "I can't trust".

I will not go into all the disruptive events in the patient's history, although a word like disruption implies, even linguistically, the quality of 'rupture' in poorly managed times of change. What was most noticeable here was that the patient described her compulsions as 'a monster'. This weighed heavily during the second part of the seminar process, when the students were asked to reflect on their impressions and put forth their considerations and questions. Many of their ideas and questions had to do with getting rid of the monster, or at least shrinking it if possible.

In the seminar format, the third step involves me (and/ or my colleague) sitting in a small circle with four or five students, surrounded by the rest of the students, the patient, and the patient's therapist. In this smaller circle, we consider our impressions, perspectives, and hypotheses garnered from the genogram and the open forum questions. The Norwegian, Tom Andersen, who developed this approach, called these groups 'reflecting teams'. The patient is present as the situation is respectfully discussed from various viewpoints (a different therapeutic setting might involve a couple or a whole family instead of a single patient). The intention is to reintroduce breadth and depth into what is often a narrow interpretation and understanding of reality, and to increase awareness of a more complex range in the potential for change. I will return to this topic later.

In this particular case, the structure of the reflecting team at last gave me a chance to express my discomfort with the one-sided version of the disease as monster. To me it appeared just as meaningful to look at the compulsive perfectionism and orderliness as a response to these three family disruptions and the resulting chaos. The family had been able to survive these blows of fate by vowing never to allow that to happen again. It is easy to see that the underlying assumption might be that nothing is dependable unless it is well planned and can be kept under control. The 'monster', therefore, can also be seen as a kind of protector against the greater monster of chaos. Although the patient's symptoms may be questionable (in both senses of the word) they do function to provide safety through 'control'.

Another patient suffering from a compulsive disturbance presented an even more conspicuous example of this kind of control. This was a man in his forties who, among other symptoms, was only able to move forward stiffly, on rigid legs, with tiny shuffling steps. It was only looking at this extreme example that it become truly clear to us what an enormous act of trust is involved in the simple movement of walking. We have to repeatedly let our body fall forward in the knowledge and trust that our legs will catch us again. When such trust is absent and someone is not prepared to fall forward in this way, the only option, anatomically, is to take tiny, stiff-legged, shuffling steps. However, everybody knows that, contrary to the intention in this case, standing and walking with stiff legs makes a person very vulnerable and much more unstable than a more adaptive, flexible stance.

It became clear in our case of the woman with the compulsive problems, that it would not necessarily be the most promising approach to try to do battle with this mechanism for security and control, this 'monster' as the patient called it—joined all too eagerly by the students. Normal methods of combat include a large dose of 'more security' and 'tighter controls,' which would mean adding even more of the same! An attempt to combat the problem with more of the same is a prime example, particularly in systemic literature, of problems being maintained, if not actually caused, by attempts to solve them. Insomnia often results from an effort to make yourself fall asleep quickly. For example, you might need a good night's sleep in order to be rested and fresh for an exam in the morning. You become more and more agitated (and awake) as the time you need for sleep ticks away and the approaching exam becomes more and more threatening. Another example is an attempt to force a spontaneous, unselfconscious smile, which is usually a fiasco and visibly false.

Monsters, too, want to be valued for their contributions and achievements in the life-process. It is only when blind attacks against the monsters have been discontinued and their actual achievements have been acknowledged, that it is possible to consider other methods of reaching the same goals. When the functions of the monster have been acknowledged, and the goals reached through some other means, there is less need for the monster to continue to be active. Only then does it become possible for it to withdraw. Of course this is a lot easier to describe than it usually is in the practice of the therapeutic process. In this context we do not intend to provide a detailed description of a specific therapeutic treatment, but more to point out a basic principle; individuals are not necessarily able to utilize the opportunities for change that may emerge from upheaval. On the contrary, the effect is often increased rigidity. Although it may be monster-like and may result in pathological symptoms, this rigidity cannot simply be fought off. We must first understand its function and what has been accomplished, and then look for alternative ways to take over these functions and their benefits.

When confronted with such a 'monster' response to (or as a result of) a major upheaval, we curiously tend to react with even tighter controls and a stronger need for order. We are then essentially feeding the monster, rather than trying to relegate it to a less central place by understanding its importance. The same is also true at a societal level. Changes produce fear, especially those radical changes that occur suddenly and unexpectedly. It is tempting to cling to an old order, even when we intuitively know that the conditions suitable to the old orders have already changed, as have the things we are trying to control. It is also tempting to call out the forces of order such as the military or police, or at least a lawyer. Aren't we confronted on all sides by the basic message that without orderly intervention, the result will be chaos, anarchy, or disaster?

Using Order and Control to Prevent Chaos

We might examine the question of our almost automatic responses in everyday life, especially in times of radical change. We grasp at control mechanisms that all too easily lead towards compulsive control, an attempt to maintain order that eventually subjects us to being controlled by the structure instead of providing a mechanism that we can use with competence.

In "Chaos, Angst und Ordnung" (Kriz 1997) I have tried to show that one fundamental reason for turning towards control mechanisms is to help us overcome our fear of helplessness. As in the case of this patient, we can understand and honor the agonizing symptoms as an effort to avert a much greater crisis. In reality, it is absolutely essential for us to develop a capacity for creating a felt sense of order in the world. The structures of our Lebenswelt have been wrested from chaos only with great difficulty. Modern natural sciences, particularly in chaos and systems theories, represent a worldview that is based on the phenomenon of a dynamic, process-oriented series of unique moments woven into an endlessly complex evolutionary process. Interestingly enough, this view of the world turns out to be congruent with the lore and wisdom of many different cultures in many different ages. As Heraclites said so many years ago, "You cannot step twice into the same river."

We could not live in our cognitive environment if our basic experience was determined by such a complete lack of structure, or such overwhelming complexity. We would experience pure panic. This was discussed in chapter 2 by citing the sociologist Peter Berger who has described a poignant scene of the human struggle at the edges of chaos.

If we ask how order is created out of chaos, the answer begins in the phylogenies. Life is already programmed to create order out of the endless complexity of a unique continuing evolution. Even prior to conceptualization and language, as an essential and organizing part of what we call culture, this "chaos avoidance" (see chapter 2) is also built into the evolutionary programming of human beings. Gestalt psychologists, for example, discovered how strongly our experience of the world is actively organized, at the deepest levels of perception, in an urge to structure 'gestalts'. Dots on a paper are automatically transformed into shapes and pictures; a series of tones will be interpreted as a melody whenever possible; and individual components (the dots or tones) take on new and specific meanings within the organization, for example, the leading note of a melody. Gestalt psychologists and others have studied countless variations in the creation of more complex structures of order.

In certain circumstances, for example, moving geometric figures can call up a convincing impression of typical 'social relationships', or 'cause and effect relationships'. This is a response that occurs even when we know it is not so. For example, if a flowerpot falls from the fourth floor balcony as you ring the doorbell of a house, you are not only startled, but you feel an immediate sense of causality. The feeling reaction is usually quickly corrected and dismissed as nonsense, but the immediate experience occurs first. In addition, there is usually a considerable quantity of stress hormones released that go on working in the body for a while afterwards. The feeling of causality has an impact even when it is imaginary and 'objectively' baseless.

The primary support and means of differentiation in this human evolutionary programming are cognitive tools and the structures of language. These help us to look into our world of experiences to find regularities, causalities, social structures and other forms of order or, as a last resort, to invent order. By creating categories and naming them, the situations and things become equivalent to one another and at the same time they lose certain aspects of their uniqueness. Strictly speaking, there has never been an evening in the history of the universe that was identical to any other evening, and no two mornings have ever been exactly alike. Still, it is not only sensible to be able to talk about morning and evening, but it is essential in our lives to be able to draw conclusions from the sequence of such categories. The sequence of day and night, ebb and flood, spring, summer, autumn and winter, and so on, are meaningful in the development and organization of our lives. The sequence of categories and their repetition is what makes it possible for us to predict and plan and to reduce the degree of uncertainty in our dealings with the world. Without a grasp of regularities, we would scarcely be able to conduct our business and activities on any given day.

Through abstractions drawn from direct sensory experience, we discover and create order, which allows us to reduce uniqueness and complexity to comprehensible categories. Holding them with names and concepts gives us the sense of trust in our world that is needed for our multi-faceted activities. When many situations seem familiar to us, we can rely on the familiarity and we have the time and freedom of mind to turn to new tasks. Just imagine what it would be like if each morning you had to negotiate every aspect of every task for the coming day with your spouse or partner. Imagine if you had to agree anew to every designation of responsibility, decisions about how to live together, goals to be set, assignment of tasks with the children, shopping, errands, and so on. One day would probably be too short to renegotiate and solve the aspects of life that have become routine over the years. If we had to do this anew every day, it would most likely occupy all our time and we would never get around to anything else. The everyday routine that we trust and take for granted is essential and it relieves us of an enormous burden.

Of course this is only one side, but it is an aspect that is central to our capacity for discovering and creating order. In therapy, on the other hand, we more often have to deal with the flip side, when the ability to create a sense of order has become pathological for a client. What appears all too familiar may warp his view of reality and his potential to experience it. However, we are not so different from our clients. Often the categories that we use to organize and describe typical situations have a more powerful impact than our actual experience of new aspects of a situation. It takes only a slight cue or hint for someone to believe that everything is already clear. A certain look, or the first word out of their partner's mouth acts as a trigger that sets off an inner reel of film. All consequent reactions are reactions to imagined assumptions and presumptions, but are unconsciously accepted as external reality. The person involved is rarely moved to question or check out these assumptions.

It is even worse when one partner discovers that much of the time, regardless of what he or she says and does, it prompts exactly the same reaction because the other person is not really listening. The first partner will then make less of an effort to try anything new or different. In turn, this serves to confirm to the other that he or she was right all along to think that it is always the same old thing. "Why change if my partner doesn't notice anything anyway?" This vicious circle between interpretation and behavior continually re-confirms itself, but also constricts the range and freedom of action. Flexibility that is not seen or acknowledged shrinks even further. Eventually, even an outside observer will be able to observe not only rigid categories and interpretations, but also rigid interactive behavior patterns. Individual and interactive dynamics are interconnected.

In short, our ability to think abstractly, to categorize, and to discover (or invent) regularities and order has proven to be a double edged evolutionary inheritance. On the one hand, it allows us to trust and make predictions; it creates a sense of security and dependability, releasing our time and energy for new activities. On the other hand, our predictions or anything that is overly familiar and dependable may block our vision of what is new and of any potential for change. Instead of profiting from increased freedom, we then experience a loss of freedom as the vicious circle tightens into increasingly restricted experiential categories and behavioral options, particularly in social relationships. The result is a loss of spontaneity, creativity, and flexibility.

The description itself, however, already provides a signpost pointing the way out of the compulsive disturbance, and it is an approach that is open to therapists from a wide variety of therapeutic orientations. The task is to reintroduce more complexity and uniqueness into the restricted categories of awareness and definitions. Since our categories are coined to a large degree by linguistic tools, the goal is to deconstruct and destabilize descriptions that are restrictive and rigid. As new possible interpretations and implications open up, they have a direct effect on awareness and behavior.

For example, consider what happens if parents choose a term such as 'behavior disorder' to describe their child to a counselor. The definition itself is static and inflexible. When they say, "our little Hans has a behavior disorder", certain kinds of narrow questions arise. "How long has he had that?" Or, "Who did he inherit this from?" It transmits an implicit image of a 'thing.' Psychologists, social scientists, and language specialists speak of 'reification.' Such a description of the problem is likely to hinder change in the actual dynamics of awareness and behavior, even though it is already clear, intuitively, that the description does not encompass the whole truth.

The first step towards softening rigidity in the descriptive language would be a formulation such as "Hans behaves in a disturbed way." Although the second description seems practically the same as the first, it opens up questions such as, "When does he behave this way and when not?" or "In what situations does he act this way, and where not?" The discussion that arises from these questions weaves all the various situations into a more complex picture in which Hans's 'disturbance' becomes comprehensible. There may be situations in which his behavior appears to be a natural reaction to provocation from his sister. In other situations, it could be a signal asking for more attention. Sometimes, it might serve to distract attention away from conflict between his parents. Of course, there will certainly also be situations in which he is simply, outrageously impossible. The important point, however, is to move beyond the constraints of the label and concept of 'behavior disorder' and restore awareness of the complexity and breadth of the situations and their significance.

Insofar as this is successful, it establishes a basis for a more differentiated awareness of the situation, which allows the parents to react in a variety of ways. In a best-case scenario, different reactions on the part of the parents may allow little Hans more room to change his behavior. The parents may have intuitively felt all along that there were sometimes other interpretations of their son's behavior, but the concept of 'a behavior disorder' focused their attention exclusively on this single 'cause' in Hans.

The Power of Language

The above example illustrates the power of language and how our cognitive structures may be greatly restricted or hardened by implicit (or explicit) linguistic categories, concepts and metaphors. The effects extend far beyond concepts such as "behavior disorder". More importantly, in our culture it is typically the big questions and topics that act as "meaning-attractors", as cognitive field forces that constrict our subjective understanding of the world and obscure our view of potential solutions. I am talking about those fundamentally important, usually value-laden questions and issues that provide us with our orientation: right or wrong, good or bad, healthy or sick, innocent or guilty, true or false, and so on. It is already clear from these examples how typically our cognitive landscape is marked by dichotomies through the use of such terms.

These polarized areas of enquiry are all meaningful, since it of course matters to us whether we can consider a statement true or false, or if someone is to be seen as guilty or innocent. Alongside this important values' orientation, however, we need to bear in mind that those questions usually relate to complex situations and developments and cannot be answered simply and decisively. Evaluative qualities such as guilty, sick, or evil depend upon the values we assign to many individual aspects. Even questions of truth, rightness, and so on are embedded in the complexities of everyday life, in processes that are difficult to define, and subject to various interpretations. They lie beyond the range of abstract, logical, mental gymnastics, where definite answers are often possible.

Although these questions can only be discussed within the constraints imposed by their complexity and the associated relativity, we discover a shocking totalitarianism in many cases, particularly in relationships that have become pathological. There are battles for survival—sometimes almost literally—in an attempt to settle such questions once and for all. "He is simply evil!" Or, "You are lying!" Often predicated by 'always', 'never', 'completely', and so on, such formulations are distortions. In addition, they often refer to reified characteristics such as, "It's just how he is!" Thought and linguistic processes of this kind hamper creativity and reduce spontaneous fluctuations in the constructed world of families and couples, particularly when the patterns of interaction would be described as rigid and encrusted.

Here, the task of therapy (as in the 'behavior disorder' example) is to deconstruct rigid descriptions, that is, to destabilize reified understanding to allow for the emergence of new interpretations that are inherent in the system. It should be noted that in most cases, and in most therapeutic approaches, we utilize language to initiate a cognitive corrective. But here language is used for the purpose of broadening understanding and increasing options for behavior. In some cases these may be categories, concepts, and metaphors that cross boundaries to create new models that project into the future and bring movement back into life. It is very difficult in most cases to find such aspects and even more difficult to name them. Another option, as illustrated in the example above, is to simply connect multiple paths of understanding with multiple situations. This breaks open the tunnel vision that stays almost hypnotically fixated on abstract categories, and opens our eyes to a bit of the fireworks of unique moments that make up our lives.

Referring to the effective power of language, our example leads us back to the macro processes that contain the discussed micro processes of therapy. We do not find our categories, concepts, and metaphors on our own, in isolated, quiet cells. On the contrary, we use those offered by society.

The Ideology of Control in Western Scientific Tradition

It is worth noting that there is reportedly a particularly strong tendency towards order, reduction and reification of processes in western culture. In his book "The Geography of Thought," Richard Nisbett (2003) emphasizes the marked differences in thinking and in consciousness between peoples of the West (mainly Europeans and Americans) and the East (Japanese and Chinese). He finds that Easterners are more holistically attuned. They think less often in categories, and more dialectically, seeking a "middle way" between opposing thoughts. Asian children learn verbs more easily than substantives, which is exactly the opposite from us. In the West we focus more on particular objects or persons in our surroundings and look for attributes with which we can order these into categories. In addition, formal logic and conceptualizing in opposites plays a much greater role in western than in eastern thought.

Nisbett looks back to differences already visible in the culture at the time of Aristotle on the one side, and Confucius on the other. I would grant the validity of much of his evidence and many of his experiments and arguments, but I believe that our culture, especially during the scientific revolution 350 years ago, experienced a thrust in a particular direction that has allowed our ideology of control to take over. That marked the beginning of what we now call western science, or sometimes—with cultural egocentricity—simply 'science'.

Along with the many obvious achievements of these scientific endeavors, we can also now see some of the disadvantages and limitations. We have favored an approach to the world that sacrifices alternatives; we have chosen one that focuses on a static, mechanistic view instead of dynamic process and that encourages analytic dissection rather than holistic observation. Particularly problematic in this view is that people are placed opposite and separate from the objects of their investigation. This blurs the motives and problems concerning the relationship of people to their objects, and personal responsibility can be concealed behind the postulates of objectivity.

This fragmenting approach to all of nature, and eventually even to our fellow human beings, reveals an inability to encounter the world in a fearless manner. Instead, by fragmenting the world, an individual need not acknowledge motives, values, or decisions, but can wrap them all in a cloak of objectivity. Abraham Maslow, one of the founders of humanistic psychology in the middle of the 20th century, interpreted this attitude as a defense against fear. In his book, "The Psychology of Science", for example, he speaks of the "pathology of recognition" and stresses the "anxiety reducing mechanisms of knowledge." In one chapter, we find a list of 21 'pathological...primarily anxiety-related' forms of our need to acquire knowledge, to know, and to understand. In a further chapter Maslow states: "Science... can be a defense. It can be primarily a philosophy of safety, a security system, a complicated way of avoiding anxiety and upsetting problems. In the extreme instance it can be a way of avoiding life, a kind of self-cloistering. It can become—in the hands of some people, at least—a social institution with primarily defensive, conserving functions, ordering and stabilizing rather than discovering and renewing." (c.f. Maslow 1966)

Maslow's formulations may appear provocative and extreme, but those proclivities are already unmistakably observable in the origins of western scientific thought. For evidence, we need only consider the 'fathers' of western science, Francis Bacon, René Descartes and Isaac Newton:

Bacon promoted the experimental method, and we find images in his work such as, "to keep nature suspended on tenterhooks until she confesses her secrets," "set the dogs on her in her torturous paths," and "tame and enslave her." These metaphors are reminiscent, not accidentally, of the witch-hunts during the reign of King James I. 'As Lord Chancellor to the king, Bacon knew only too well about that procedure. In the history of ideas, not only have witches been burned, but also alternatives to the incipient 'scientific' knowledge and the archaic access to nature have been deliberately suppressed, if not completely eradicated.

In Descartes' school of thought, his differentiation between res cogitans and res extensa (loosely formulated, between the world of the mind and the material world) led to organisms not only being compared to machines, but also to them being treated like mere machines. About 1700, Nicola Fontaine reported that in the Cartesian

School of Port-Royal, animals were nailed to boards and dissected alive. Their cries were regarded by the researchers as nothing more than the noise of clock works. Even worse, those who attributed feelings of pain to animals were ridiculed as 'unscientific'. When we consider the fact that human infants and children most typically respond with anthropomorphic identification and feelings (they normally react to screams or crying with those same expressions), the adult scientists must have had to erect remarkable defenses to block out this response. This is tragically reminiscent of pious Americans' justification for the use and abuse of slaves. 'Niggers' were not considered humans and were therefore exempt from the dictates of the Bible to "love thy neighbor as thyself." It also recalls the murder of millions of Jews in German concentration camps by those who have otherwise been described as loving family men. Reduced awareness and defense mechanisms are still seen today in incidents of torture throughout the world. This act is psychologically possible only when one's Lebenswelt is structured so that the individual stands separate from an observed and analyzed object and does not encounter or identify with the 'other' in any way—certainly not as a fellow human being.

Isaac Newton, a leading figure in the development of western scientific thought, stressed the importance of mathematical abstractions and categorical generalizetions. From this point of view, a unique moment or object only has meaning and value as an example of a generalization. As Maslow emphasized, individual examples are anonymous and expendable, not unique or sacrosanct. They have no individual value in their own right. As we have already determined, categorical generalization provides the basis for regularities and therefore for prediction and control, which help us to reduce our anxiety about what is continuously new and unpredictable.

For about three hundred years, this approach to the world and the metaphors of western scientific thought have permeated all aspects of our everyday life and have become a general world view that is rarely called into question. We tend to satisfy our natural need for security exclusively through controlling order. This has expanded beyond the realm of things to apply to relationships with other people as well, and finally to our relationship to ourselves. Accordingly, even in the field of psychotherapy, we find many more programs today promoting self-control or self-management, than any encouraging self-confidence. Loss of control is more likely to be seen as pathological and threatening than is a loss of confidence.

At the same time however, it appears to us that this one- sided coping strategy of oversimplification and abstraction (even extending to natural life processes and feelings), has proven increasingly inadequate. Our western, technological card of control and safety has been trumped. As I mentioned initially, a few fanatics with a box knife were able to bring down not only the symbol of the economic power of the West, but also one of our most well protected buildings, the Pentagon. Remarkably enough, the Twin Towers collapsed so quickly after the attack because of, not in spite of, the seemingly perfect engineering. The structurally ingenious steel construction was particularly susceptible to conditions of extreme heat.

Recent accidents involving high speed trains, tunnel catastrophes (despite outstanding engineering), breakdowns in nuclear reactors, and so on, all demonstrate that it is impossible to guarantee absolute safety. However, instead of developing techniques that can adapt to unforeseen changes and errors, the focus remains primarily on a strategy of overall control and prevention of error.

An illustration of a lack of adaptability that is more annoying than threatening can be found in the current German railway system. In my personal experience of trains in Germany and Switzerland I have noticed a crucial difference in the underlying philosophy behind the timetables in the two countries. In Switzerland, trains stop at some large stations for a rather long time, up to 15 minutes or more. This allows for a cushion that can absorb shorter delays so that the correspondence between the timetables and reality is very high. Trains in Switzerland are extremely punctual, even when a change of trains is involved. The same used to be true in Germany, but for the past twenty years or so the timetables appear to have been 'optimized' by computers. To shorten journey times, stopover times have been cut as well as the time allowed for changing trains, and the train speeds have increased. This works very well on the computer, but there is no margin of error to accommodate small delays since the trains cannot drive faster, and the station stops cannot be shortened any further. Consequently, trains often run over the allowed margin of delay, and the whole timetable breaks down, including the connections with other routes. I now find it necessary to add a safety margin of at least two hours to the actual timetable and I still run the risk of not being on time! There may well be other reasons contributing to the dramatic change in Germany, but I am convinced that a little less 'optimized' efficiency and more adaptability would provide more actual efficiency.

This philosophy of efficiency through planning and optimization and an attendant disregard for reality and its disruptive effects seems to be typical on other levels and in other areas as well. While expanding our technical range and insisting that everything is under control, we concurrently run a risk of ever-greater catastrophes. Development is being driven into ever more foolhardy areas, in classical, material technology as well as biotechnology.

One price of this development is a rising threat to the first world due to the increasing gap between rich and poor, between our squandering of resources and under-development, but also due to our destruction of the fundaments of our own life through abuse of ecological systems. Even here, however, we are assured by our politicians that all these developments, the climatic catastrophes, the hole in the ozone layer, the droughts, acid rain, mountains of rubbish, nuclear waste, and so on, can eventually be brought under control.

Modern Systems Theory:
A More Adequate and Comprehensive Approach to Our Complex, Inter-related World.

Interestingly enough, some modern science is currently in the process of very radical change, and some meaningful alternatives are now being developed to the domination of western thought of the past few centuries. I am referring to an interdisciplinary systems theory that has been changing natural science over the past three decades and has even found its way into popular magazines and media with terms such as 'self-organization' and 'chaos theory.' This is due to the fact that the phenomena and discoveries of systems theory are much more relevant to our everyday life than many other earth shaking discoveries in science. At the beginning of the 20th century, our western scientific view of the world was already shaken to its foundations by developments such as relativity theory and quantum mechanics. But in fact, in everyday life, our mechanistic metaphors and views were scarcely affected, not even in most scientific endeavors. Although it was certainly unwarranted, these earthshaking discoveries were dismissed and successfully relegated to the status of extraordinary phenomena, irrelevant to our normal

Lebenswelt. They have been regarded purely as either phenomena of the macro-cosmos or as extremely micro-cosmic.

With respect to systems theory, on the other hand, scientists are now noticing with fascination that under certain circumstances even very simple mathematical equations, and those very simple systems that can be mathematically represented, are no longer predictable, which means they become chaotic. Moreover, it is increasingly recognized that this is not anything particularly exceptional in nature, but actually what is normal in a process world. In reality, the classic principles of predictability and stability are only true under rather artificially established conditions, but artificial conditions are typical of many technical constructions. In most technical areas, specific principles can usually be sufficiently isolated and applied in a controlled way, which is why classical science has been able to claim such great progress in these technical areas.

When we consider the limits of technical controllability, the essential factor is the extent to which we can sufficiently isolate the relevant phenomena. This means, to what extent we can ignore the aspect of feedback and deal with only one relatively isolated part of a system, divorced from those complex chains of effects which are normally ubiquitous in nature. For example, under relatively constant, controlled conditions, and sufficiently isolated from other processes, the firing mechanisms in a car motor will function billions of times. Similar restricttions are true in many other areas of technology. However, when dealing with complex technical systems, the conditions of isolation are seldom adequate, or are attainable only with serious theoretical or practical limitations. The justification for these constraints is even more dubious in normal life, in biology or medicine, and especially in the realm of human interactions, where complex interactions are the rule. In these areas, the classical approach of artificially isolating one piece of the process is rarely appropriate.

As a matter of fact, this helps to explain the frequent failure of one-sided plans that depend on controlling all processes instead of utilizing the support of a self-organizing process. In a recent book called "Ja, mach nur einen Plan", Stefan Strohschneider and Rüdiger von der Weth (2002) present a number of case studies that illustrate the absurdity of bureaucratic attempts to control every detail of a complex, non-technical process instead of using flexible guidelines to support self-organizing competence. In practice, the latter would be far better for promoting flexible adaptations to non-predictable, idiosyncratic events. One case in the book looks at a major fire in 1995 in a university clinic in Aachen, a building housing about eleven thousand people. The bulky file labeled "catastrophe plan," based on administrative edicts, was of very little help. There were no factual answers to the questions that needed to be dealt with in the actual situation. Much of the case study reads like satire or a collection of instances of organized foolishness. According to the authors, the containment of the catastrophe was due less to the quality of emergency planning than to pure good luck.

There are growing concerns, based on systems and chaos theories, about an increasing threat of conflict between our control bias and the uncontrollability of complex processes, particularly in typical man/machine or man/man interactions. One argument against these concerns, however, has been to cite the fact that we have managed to exist—and exist well—for a long time without worrying about such problems. Up to now, our world has clearly functioned satisfactorily. It has been, and is, possible to make predictions, and so far we have remained relatively unaffected by the supposed chaotic behavior that surrounds us, or by the limitations of systems.

Therefore, according to this argument, even though our current theoretical tools and computers are now capable of showing us the effects of chaotic dynamics, not much has changed in the real world.

But, this argument is not valid. It must be said, on the contrary, that things have indeed changed with respect to rapid industrial development and information technology. A few decades back, interventions into nature were relatively local. People were far less environmentally aware than they are today. They produced proportionally more waste and the products that were dumped were more damaging to the environment, but their actions remained relatively isolated. There was a paper mill here, a tannery there, a few hundred thousand (or million) cars that each produced more poisonous exhaust, but altogether were fewer in number and transported fewer goods across the country. Today, the large industries are complexly interconnected and produce effects that can no longer be controlled. One example of this is the impact on the self-purification systems of rivers. Interdependent relationships within the information sector are even more obvious. Television, radio, telephones, and the Internet bring almost any event from the furthest corner of the world into our living rooms within hours, minutes, or even live, as it happens. Monetary funds, stocks and bonds, commodities options are connected worldwide by telephone or on-line links. One result is that people get information through this network about, for example, preliminary preparatory steps for the introduction of some new organizational measure, and they are able to react very quickly to this information. Also, there are many more people who are immediately informed because they are connected in various ways. There are more and more channels of information and everyone can react more quickly than used to be the case. It now requires literally only a click to engage and intervene. As a consequence, important sectors of this world have changed so drastically in the past decades that the inter-connectivity of partial processes, the crucial point in chaos theory, has become a factual reality. The behavior of the system is different in reality from the classic behavior of a relatively isolated, or sufficiently isolated, part of the whole system.

At the same time, there is a powerful urge to hold on to our old, mechanistic view of the world. In the conservative ideologies of the rich and powerful, the principle of control is much more comfortable than is trust and support for the principles of self-organization. An ideology of control justifies intervention by those forces of containment, such as the military or police, to maintain order and protect the structures of power and wealth. On the contrary, allowing an increase in the self-organization of processes might bring about more beneficial solutions for the whole, but could endanger the position of those now in control.

It is no coincidence that it took almost a century before science could turn its attention from the efforts to impose controls on order and its problematic tendency to disintergrate—as posed in thermodynamics—in order to also look at an independent emergence of order, that is, the theories of systems and self-organization.

In the meantime, even lay people have become aware of problems and the unfeasibility of the principle of control in complex feedback systems. One only has to consider the pollution of air and water, famine caused by short-sighted 'developmental assistance', avalanches due to deforestation, the ecological catastrophes that we have already experienced and others that are now gathering force, national and global economic crises, or our waning euphoria about the unlimited potential of medical-technological advances. The model of cause and effect which had appeared to be adequate, is less and less convincing in a world so technically complex and interconnected, particularly in communications technology, that the effects of interventions rarely remain localized. A well-meant corrective intervention in response to a perceived problem in one area can have effects that spread through the network of connections and lead to unforeseen consequences.

There are also effects at the micro level, that is, on our state of mind. Many years ago the American psychologist, Martin Seligman, presented his widely accepted and respected concept of 'learned helplessness' to explain depression, apathy, and apparently unmotivated aggression. Supported by research with animals and humans, he concluded that such reactions emerge or are learned when there is no discernible connection between action and effects (see Seligman 1992).

To my knowledge, Seligman' research was concerned with the immediate social and material surroundings of the individuals investigated. However, it is clear that in the trend towards increasingly complex social and informational systems and their increasing inscrutability and unpredictability, a discernable connection between action and its effects is lost to the individual, in general. Therefore, the concept of learned helplessness can also be applied to this general trend. The 'no future' attitude of many young people actually means, "it does not matter what we do, we have so little influence on what happens." It seems very plausible that this could stimulate apathy and aggression. At the same time we see signs of other coping mechanisms in operation. For example, it might explain the popularity of computer games in which the success of one's actions is directly controllable (even though success all too often depends on the very questionable technique of shooting one's increasingly more realistic enemies).

The current widespread popularity of guru-types, with their simplified visions of the world, can also be seen as a coping response to increasingly unpredictable complexities in the real world and an attempt to bring it under control. When ideological leaders present simple, clear views of the world of religion, politics, economics, and unfortunately now science as well, it seems to offer an enormously attractive orientation to those who feel insecure in an overly complex world.

It seems clear that we urgently need to correct the principles and metaphors operating in politics and other hubs of decision-making in our society to correspond to the altered reality of the world. We have to relinquish our increasingly inadequate, life-threatening principles—those principles based on a mechanical view of the world—because they are not appropriate to highly complex, interconnected, and dynamic systems. As I have indicated, and as we all experience every day, this is no simple task. The three hundred years of development in western scientific thought and its world altering products go hand in hand with that pervasive mechanistic ideology that depends most highly on control, and generates a fear of non-linear, volatile, unpredictable dynamics. Those dynamics, however, are typical of creative development and healing processes as well as many other processes in our lives and could be experienced more intensely if they were not held in check by the control mechanisms of our culture.

On the one hand, current upheavals in our world have their locus in material-social structures, where we have created an enormous degree of complexity of interconnectedness—broadly termed globalization. On the other hand, however, they are also of an ideological nature. A significant aspect of discussions and disagreements within and between various social structures seems to me to be an ideological controversy between two cultures of thought.

On the one hand, we have a culture that continues to one-sidedly follow the classic principles of control, capability, objectivity and predictability. On the other hand lies a culture that emphasizes a more holistic and process orientation to the world, one that observes and supports natural developments. In addition, upheavals in the macro processes of society are closely interwoven with the micro processes at an individual and family level in the structures of meaning and narrative.

Systemic Flexibility in Times of Radical Change

In the context of systemic psychotherapy with individuals, couples, and families, and in coaching for individuals and organizations, we know that instituting more control, tighter restrictions, and more careful planning does not offer a solution for overcoming rigid dynamics, a narrow understanding of problems, or an inability to initiate change. It is more productive to support the processes of self-organization that are often present to an astounding degree, even in highly organized and hierarchical organizations (Kriz 2003).

It is crucial to attend to the pendulum of dynamic instability and stability—we have already mentioned the example of walking—in addition to an appreciation for uniqueness and sensory feedback. By the latter, I mean an experiential counteraction to the temptations of categorical abstractions. Whereas this cognitive reductionism is often necessary, there is a danger that in looking at individual events and concrete situations only as examples of categories, we may lose sight of the specifics and overlook long-term changes and opportunities for solutions.

In this context, I would plead for a more equal balance between the normally overemphasized planning of actions and the completely undervalued imagination.

Planning follows clearly defined aims and goals along pathways that normally preclude any deviation from the original prognosis. This is an element typical of our classical western view of the world and naturally important and productive in the appropriate context. Imagining the future, on the other hand, is a typical example of a cognitive dynamic with a systemic attraction. Moving towards a goal, perhaps some professional aim, we have only a vague idea about the concrete realization. For example, if one wants to become a professional psychologist, it is rather vague at the beginning of one's studies what the job will really look like in five years. Moving towards this vague goal, however, there are decisions to be made along the way that then clarify the goal.[3]

This process of approaching a goal leaves room for creative and flexible adaptation to the givens, but also to unforeseen developments, changes, and disruptions in peripheral conditions. On such a path, deviations pose no difficulties and will not be seen as unpleasant surprises standing in the way of some precisely defined plan. On the contrary, even major corrections to one's plans are normal and to be expected. Instead of controlling the plans and goals and trying to avoid diversions, detours and surprises, the main moving forces here are openness, creativity, flexibility, and a search for meaning.

It is not my intent to set one principle against the other, as both have their own justification for being, just as dynamics and stability are oppositional but equally neces-

---

[3] This corresponds to modern systems theory: The attractors become clearer and more detailed and precise as the attractive dynamic develops the system in the direction of these attractors (see Kriz 1999, 2001)

sary. I do, however, wish to critically question a one-sided emphasis on planning in preference to imagination. It is precisely in times of upheaval and change that flexibility and creativity are more likely to be appropriate and successful than the controlled security of precisely defined plans.

A stronger appreciation of imaginative strength rather than forces of domination requires a clearer acknowledgement of values. In my opinion, those in power today lack the courage to develop imagination or to expound the attendant values. In Germany, this reluctance may have something to do with earlier abuses and the betrayal of values in the history of the 20th century. I am not pleading for an institutional or governmental definition of values; what is required is a discursive dialogue of differing positions. From the viewpoint of existential philosophy, people have to create their future, and the discussion of imaginative goals, orientation, and values is undeniably important. The well-known Viennese psychotherapist, Victor Frankl, was a specialist in the search for the meaning of life. In his report of his experiences in a concentration camp, he referred to Nietzsche's statement "One who has a why in life, can bear almost any how" (Frankl 1984). This 'why' also implicitly contains an imaginative-teleological 'for what' and, therefore, an orientation towards values.

When there is such an orientation towards goals and meanings, imaginatively embedded in the complex totality, upheaval need not lead to fearful rigidity or controlling compulsions. The changes may be experienced as necessary, even life-enhancing transitions and as opportunities for transformation. A mini 'die and become' allows rigid structures to adapt to new conditions and demands.

I would wish for all of us the courage, capacity, and trust to face upheaval and change in this creative way.

References

Frankl, V. (1984) Man's search for Meaning. New York: Simon & Schuster

Kriz, J. (1997) Chaos, Angst und Ordnung, Göttingen: Vandenhoeck

Kriz, J. (1999) On Attractors - The Teleological Principle in Systems Theory, the Arts and Therapy in: POIESIS. A Journal of the Arts and Communication.

Kriz, J. (2001):Self-Organization of Cognitive and Interactional Processes. In: Matthies, M., Malchow, H. & Kriz, J (Eds): Integrative Systems Approaches to Natural and Social Dynamics. Heidelberg: Springer, 517-537

Kriz, J. (2003) Selbstorganisationsprozesse in Organisationen: Von Senge's »Kochrezepten« zu den Grundlagen des Kochens – oder: auf dem Weg zu einer systemtheoretischen Fundierung des Coaching. In: Hamborg, Kay & Holling, Heinz (Hg.) Innovative Personal und Organisationsentwicklung. Göttingen: Hogrefe, S. 186–210.

Maslow, A. (1966) The Psychology of Science. New York: Harper & Row

Nisbett, R. (2003) The Geography of Thought. New York/London: The Free Press

Seligman, M. (1992) Helplessness: On depression, development, and death. New York: Freeman

Strohschneider, S., von der Wet, R. (2002) Ja, mach nur einen Plan [Yes, just make a plan], Bern: Hans Huber (2nd ed.)

.

Chapter **4**

THE RE-ENCHANTMENT
OF OUR WORLD

CHAOS AND STRUCTURE AS THE BASIS
OF OUR MODERN WORLD VIEW

This essay—published in 2003 in German—is a written version of the opening address given at the 2002 Conference on Psychosocial Oncology (congress theme: "Chaos and Structure in Psychosocial Oncology").

I was asked by the organizers to give a more general introduction to some of the fundamental concepts of chaos and systems theory which was not too scientific or mathematical. Therefore I tried to formulate an invitation to think about the ideas involved in order to provide the audience with the concepts they need to take part in this growing interdisciplinary discourse.

The following chapter serves the same purpose in the context of this book.

"Chaos" and "structure" were central themes of that annual meeting. In many announcements of the lectures and workshops and in other publications of Psychosocial Oncology, "chaos" is referred to on three different levels:

First of all, on the somatic level, chaos it is seen in "chaotic cell growth". Second, on the psychological level, we find this theme with respect to the "inner chaos of the patient's experience". And third, on the organisational level, people in the field of Psychosocial Oncology often report the "chaos in the interaction structure" of the very institutions which they are woven into—as patients or as professional helpers. It is a chaos which often leaves them feeling helpless.

In all three perspectives, chaos has a rather negative connotation. Clearly, for many people, the diagnosis "cancer" breaks unexpectedly into their Lebenswelt,[1] in which chaos, particularly in the form of death or severe suffering, seemed until then to be present at the very most on the fringes. In some cases, it is often completely suppressed beyond the cognitive boundaries of everyday awareness.

It is no wonder then that the violence with which this experience now breaks in to the Lebenswelt gives rise to an equally violent scenario in the exposure to this threatening illness. Psychotherapists know how much and how often the symptoms of patients are mirrored in the interaction structures—particularly in supervision groups.

It is therefore understandable when the malignant, violent, gladiatorial and displacing aspects of the cancer dynamic develop a tendency to afflict the interaction dynamic as well.

Similarly, this negative connotation of "chaos" has also been widely used in Psychopathology and psychotherapy. From C.G. Jung to the modern phenomenological discussions about schizophrenia, we find the theme of the threat that is posed to human experience by chaotic randomness. Many clinical psychologists have described

---

[1] life world or personal world of experiences

the great fear experienced by a person who finds himself at the mercy of unpredictable events and the collapse of trusted structures.

But chaos need not only be connected with negative connotations. In the following, the positive aspects of chaos, which are all too often over-looked, will be brought back into focus. The argument will be elaborated in three steps:

In the first step, the classical world view of the nineteenth century, and its changes as a result of modern chaos theory (as a part of systems research), are described. This classical world view is very important. Through the progress of technology and its influence on education, this view governs our current everyday understanding of "the world"—and thus also the understanding of phenomena like "life", "illness", "change", "development" etc. In addition, this view determines our relationship to the objects and living beings of the world to a great extent—and furthermore, our relationship to other human beings and, finally, to oneself. As a consequence, our language is full of classical mechanistic metaphors even with regard to the processes of life. And these metaphors have a determining influence on the world view and understanding of patients, therapists, and professional helpers, too.

The second step will introduce some central findings about "chaos and structure" from the modern natural sciences. Only the "bare facts" are presented here. However, this may not only illuminate the reasons why countless scientists from various disciplines are so fascinated with work on this theme. Moreover, these principles of modern systemic natural sciences seem to be much more adequate for the understanding of psychological and interactional processes than many old mechanistic principles that still govern present day psychology and psychotherapy.

Therefore, in the third step, we will return to the level of phenomenology and experience, and will discuss the meaning of the reported findings, as well as the change to the world view for everyday life. From this discussion, new perspectives for the understanding of "our world"—and especially the experience of our Lebenswelt—may result.

Thematically, a rather long journey is taken in these three steps. As with all such journeys carried out in a limited time, it is generally advisable to take a bird's eye view, and to take a flight over the landscape (which is, here, a cognitive one). In doing so, many of the details may become fuzzy. But we do get an overview—and it is not forbidden to allow oneself to use other opportunities to take a closer look at certain parts of the landscape (for example, to refer to one of the many books about the underlying themes involved).

The Classical Disenchantment of the World

The Lebenswelt of the people in ancient times and the middle ages was, to a great extent, "enchanted". This was not only because there were sorcerers and witches—people who were concerned with actively opposing the emerging rationalist explanation of the world with alternative approaches.[2] Many things in the Lebenswelt were endowed with a "soul".[3] This meant that these things were granted individuality instead of being predominantly seen as arbitrary examples for more general categories. As a

---

[2] The widespread eradication of these people coincided with the emergence of modern science.
[3] This was taken up again later in the Romantic Age, but then had only a minor influence on the already developed modern sciences.

consequence, the uniqueness of things and situations characterized the world of experience.

In those times, in the pursuit of knowledge, and also in scientific activities, the point was to remain in accordance with nature, and not to primarily control and change it. This happened naturally against the backdrop of a divine order, which should be identified by human activities (or rather: re-identified, in the sense of the Platonic Ideals). Discovery of the order of the divine, of knowledge of the world, and of insight of self were different aspects of the same mental attitude, and thus went hand in hand. For example, the processes of purification of materials in the field of alchemy in order to produce the "Philosopher's Stone" or gold were also meant at the same time as psycho-spiritual processes. This holistic unity of the world, discussed under the term *unus mundus*, was mirrored, for example, in the mathematics of Pythagoras. His notion of the "harmonices mundi"—the divine harmony of the universe—was later the guiding principle for Kepler's mathematical description of the movements of the planets. The distances between the planetary orbits also reflected this divine harmony in the natural intervals of music, as well as in the structure of geometry: it is generally known that the orbits of the known planets (first conceptualized as circles) at that time seemed to be surprisingly exact in their agreement with the relationships between the Platonic bodies (tetrahedrons, cubes, etc.).

This unity of the world, its associated enchantment and the security experienced by people regarding this magic, fit aptly into the context of Ptolemy's world view. Accordingly, typical drawings of this world view present man and "his" earth at rest within the shell of the planets, like the chick in the egg or the embryo in the mother's belly: cared for, safe and secure.

However, this world-view—endorsed by the Occidental Church—didn't just offer security to the people; it was also a source of the misuse of power and paternalism. In the emancipation from these claims of power and authority during the Age of Enlightenment, the world was disenchanted. At the same time, there was the emergence of what we call "science" in the present understanding in our culture. Correspondingly, not only the sorcerers and witches, but also the science of Alchemy and many other alternative approaches to the understanding of our world, were fought against, quashed, and exterminated. This was discussed with respect to the rise of modern science and its experimental methods already in chapter 3.

The emerging modern sciences with their empirical and experimental methods, mathematically analysed, understood the world more and more as a clockwork mechanism. As well as dismissing the idea of the "Creator", the Enlightenment had also rendered the creative aspects of our world superfluous (at least in the area of science). Pierre de Laplace's famous metaphor of the "demon" makes this point clear: provided that a demon at some point in time could determine the positions and velocities of all particles and their effective energies, he could, according to de Laplace, determine the past and future of all of the appearances and phenomena in the whole universe, with complete certainty. Such a world, thought of as clockwork, may be highly detailed and very complicated. However, every possibility of a creative or non-deterministic development and unfolding of the world is ultimately denied.

De Laplace, who well represented the hubris of the 19th century scientist, also discredited Kepler as a religious fool. He heavily discredited Kepler's idea of the *harmonices mundi*, which ascribed a particular meaning to the structure of the planetary orbits. According to De Laplace, on the other hand, the Newtonian conception of natural laws much better represents reality. In this approach distinguished orbits do not make any sense—every planetary constellation, provided it complies with Newtonian laws, is possible and equivalent.

This is an example of the implicit assumptions of analysis, synthesis, and homogeneity, which basically governed classical thinking: a complex phenomenon (like the planetary system) is decomposed—analytically, and (where possible) even experimentally. The resulting parts were then joined synthetically together back into a whole. This, of course, functions only when a certain homogeneity is assumed, i.e. when the whole is nothing more than the "sum of the parts" (and here I allude to alternative conceptions, as pointed out in particular by Gestalt Psychology). In addition, it is necessary to assume that the parts are homogeneously interchangeable and do not hold any value as individual unique entities.

This thinking still affects our world view and our ways of dealing with things today to a great extent. For example, many people favour concrete for building, instead of using natural stones which each have an individual structure. To use stones instead of concrete seems to be a painstaking business. Therefore, stones were crushed ("analysis") and their individual structures are stripped away. These homogeneous parts are then almost arbitrarily pliable, and synthetically joined back together into concrete. The same can be seen with the intrinsic structure of wood when it is processed into hardboard. In supermarkets, one has long been able to find so-called "reformed meat", which is similarly analytically-synthetically processed. And one could consider whether similar principles underlie genetic engineering, or the search for the "effective factors" in psychotherapy. Many people dream of the synthesis of an "optimally formed" psychotherapy—created from homogenous effective factors found in the different psychotherapeutic schools when scientists have eroded the uniqueness and intrinsic value of these approaches.

Therefore, in spite of all the comforts gained by science and its technology and engineering through the disenchantment of the world, we should still be critical. The procedure of abstracting general categories with homogenous parts from unique phenomena is a special approach which, however, cannot be adopted to all problems and phenomena. The reduction of complexity through abstraction in order to control everything is especially arbitrary when applied to processes of life, psychological phenomena and social interactions. But the tendency to meet people's natural need for security unilaterally through the control of order, is so strong in our society that it even shows itself in human relationships—in the interactions and encounters with self, others, and the world at large. Accordingly, in psychotherapy we find many more programs for the promotion of self-control (in particular self-management), than for self-confidence. And the "loss of control" is more often discussed in psychopathological literature and is more feared than the "loss of confidence".

Today, we know from modern systems theory that Kepler was at least as correct as Newton: nature is in no way as homogenous as was still believed until recently. There are, in fact, distinguished planetary orbits. Many other structures and distances between the planetary orbits are indeed possible, but not just any one: If one simply takes orbits at random (which all conform to Newton's laws), then in many cases, the "whole"—the planetary system –becomes instable and collapses as a result of resonance effects between the planets. And it is also not true that "nature does not make leaps" (natura non facit saltus), as Leibniz summarised yet another aspect of the homogeneity assumption. In contrast, the basis of nature is (quantum) leaps, and today this is accepted in physics as a ruling doctrine. In addition, in the field of human sciences we have known at least since the publication of the critically dismissed book from the two once enthusiastic Skinner students Breland & Beland: "The Misbehavior of Organisms", that the idea of using operant conditioning to build up any behavior from smaller steps (i.e. to synthesize) is no longer accepted. The human will for order is also subject to such limits, that natural order—for example instinctive behavior—pays attention and must be respected.

However, these insights are already part of the re-enchantment of the world through modern science, particularly through chaos theory and systems research. Some significant aspects, which give rise to this new contemplation and reflection, will be sketched in the following section.

Some Findings Regarding Chaos and Structure

a) The (Re-)Discovery of Chaos

It is often reported that modern chaos research began with an accident around 40 years ago. At the beginning of the 60s, the Meteorologist Edward Lorenz sat at a computer at MIT (Massachusetts Institute of Technology), and tried to predict the development of the weather using a mathematical model. In order to compute the predictions of this model, Lorenz had to type initial data into computer which then calculated the changes, step by step.

After working for weeks with that model, it happened that Lorenz wanted to re-calculate a longer-term change. In order to save time, he shortened the procedure by simply re-using the figures output by an earlier, shorter-term change calculation as input. In doing so, he produced an overlap in the calculations. To his horror, however, the second-round calculations ran differently—in actual fact, completely differently—to the first time, although the model was made up of only three relatively simple equations. Lorenz first of all believed that there must have been a failure in the input of the figures. But there wasn't. His computer was also not at fault. Rather, Lorenz had stumbled across something which would change the view of our world with lasting effect—and his achievement was that he understood the great importance of his findings.

It was not just the inaccuracy of some digits of the input figures which explains the completely different development of the two calculated developments. As a matter of fact, as we now know, even 100, 1000, or 1 million places of accuracy had not, in principal, changed. The problem lay in the fact that Lorenz had used a model which had, until then, been avoided because of the amount of work involved in the calculations of such models. However, by using a brand-new computer made recently available (for non-military research), it seemed easy to do these calculations. The equations were indeed quite simple, but they were non-linear and had a feedback term, i.e., the change of a variable had some kind of effect on the change of a second variable, and vice versa.

That such cross-linking of interacting variables is found almost everywhere in the real world, was in fact evident to every scientist. However, it was long believed that a weak feedback could be disregarded. This seemed to be a meaningful assumption from the point of view of efficiency, because the use of non-linear processes is computationally expensive. In addition, our experience seemed to prove that complicated applications could be reduced with sufficient accuracy to linear changes—this belief ultimately underlay differential calculus. Figure 4.1 demonstrates in a simple way what is meant by this.

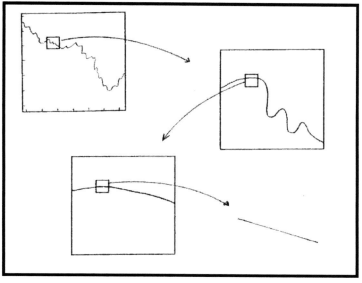

Figure 4.1 The classical conception of the approximation to linearity of an arbitrary part of a curve, with sufficiently small sections.

Admittedly, it was in principal already known long before Lorenz that our apparently so uniform nature entailed the most absurd possibilities for development. In 1887, for example, King Oscar II of Sweden offered the then considerable sum of 2,500 Krone as a prize, which the Swedish Academy of Sciences announced as: Sought is a valid answer to the question: "Is the solar system stable?"

Some decades earlier, one would have been burnt at the stake for expressing such manifest doubt as in this question. And also in 1887, this question seemed, to many people, to be impertinent or the height of nonsense, especially since the solar system and the movements and orbits of the planets were understood (and still are), as the embodiment of the eternal, the stable, the reliable. Consequently, it seemed only to be a question of more refined techniques of proof, with the goal of dispelling any doubts conclusively and with scientific exactness.

However, this then-famous "academic question" pushed the gates to the abyss of chaos wide open. Three years later, in 1890, the famous French mathematician Henri Poincaré (1854-1912) was awarded the prize in question. His award-winning work confirmed all of the prejudice and bitter experience which characterized the interactions between scientists on the one hand, and practitioners, politicians and journalists on the other hand. Instead of giving a short, clear answer to the very simply stated question "Is the Solar System stable?", Poincaré wrote 270 pages of very complicated and long-winded remarks, which in addition concluded that a deterministic answer to this question is not, as a matter of principle, possible. Strictly speaking, it was therefore not really an "answer" (at least not in the manner which practitioners, politicians and journalists believe that an "answer" should be).

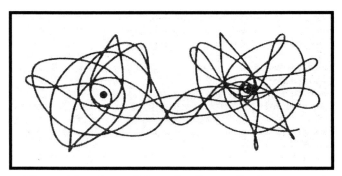

Figure 4.2a: A possible path of a small planet around two fixed stars of equal mass (from Peitgen & Richter 1986).

The reason for Poincaré's conclusion will be understandable by means of Figure 4.2a, which shows a possible path of a small planet, orbiting two heavenly bodies (e.g., fixed stars) of the same mass (therefore already quite a simplified assumption). As you may still remember from school, the entire gravitational astronomy is based upon the ability to calculate the movement of one body in relation to a second, since the so-called three body problem —or indeed the consideration of the interactions of all nine planets—is actually unsolvable. The complexity of the path (seen in Figure 4.2a) of this reduced three body problem offers an intuitive insight for the reader into the difficulties of computing a deterministic solution.

In order to give a realistic impression of these difficulties, Figure 4.2b shows a solution to this simplified three body problem from 1925, computed 35 years after Poincaré's answer. The special feature of this work is that to get this illustration, or rather its underlying data, 56 scientists worked for 15 years (or 840 man-years of calculating time!) under the leadership of the Danish Astronomer Elis Strömgren. It is understandable then that further calculations of similar—or indeed of more realistic and therefore even more complex development processes—couldn't have been expected before the dawn of the Computer Age.

Seen in a historical sense, Lorenz's discovery was in no way coincidental. It was only at the beginning of the 60s that the first generation of computers was available to those outside of the military and some development laboratories. Much of the work which was then discussed under the titles Chaos Theory or Non-linear Systems, had already been precisely mathematically stated by Poincaré, and had later, during World War I, been elaborated further by his students Gaston Julia (1893-1978) and Pierre Fatou (1878-1929). However, Lorenz was not aware that his big discovery, which was the beginning of chaos theory in the US, had already been discovered and, to a great extent, theoretically elaborated in Europe 70 years earlier. Indeed, the phenomena described by Poincaré, Julia, Fatou and others had been abandoned to the mathematical curiosity cabinet. Some of the now re-discovered and relevant structures of Fractal Geometry were even labelled as "Monsters" (cf. Kriz 1992), because some knew that these approaches and findings would change our understanding of the world.

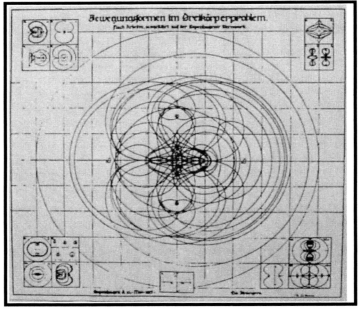

Figure 4.2b. Possible paths analogous to Figure 4.2a—from a work by E. Strömgren, 1925.

b) The Relevance of Chaos Research

At this point, the question of relevance seems to be obvious. Even if one concedes that it was first possible with today's computers to address these problems, isn't it curious that we got by for so long "without these problems"? Our world and the explanations of its dynamics have evidently "functioned" quite adequately so far.

Consequently, one could argue that predictions were, and are, possible without taking chaos theory into account. Moreover, we didn't notice very much of the reputedly chaotic behavior of the systems we encounter all around us. Although we now have computers, which quite clearly show us the chaos, it seems that nothing in the real world has actually changed!

Such obvious objections must however be countered with: Sure! Something has changed! And this does actually have something to do with the computers which make the chaos so clear to us—more precisely, with the rapid industrial development and particularly Information Technology. Only a few decades ago, interferences in nature were relatively local. People were probably much less aware of environmental issues than today, and measured in percent, threw away much more rubbish and much worse products than we do. But these activities were relatively isolated; here was a paper mill, there a tannery. There were some hundreds of thousands or just a few million automobiles, which certainly produced much more exhaust fumes individually. But compared to the situation of today, cars only existed in minor numbers and transported a lot less goods across the country. Today, we have large networked industries, which to an extent encroach upon the self-purification-system-cycle of rivers, which are no longer able to cope with this disruption.

Even more clearly however, we experience the interconnectedness in the Information Sector. The media—

particularly television, radio and telephone—bring events from the furthest corners of the world to us in our homes, within hours, or even minutes. Foreign exchange transactions, equity trading, and goods options are moved over internationally networked telephones or even directly by computer. "Market competitors" also find out about the preparation and scheduling of the introduction of new organisational actions as a result of this information networking, and can react much faster with well-directed measures. And a great deal more "participants", who are involved in some way in the overall process, can be reached faster and through more information channels. As a consequence, they can then intervene back into the shared system, in ways which were earlier not as conceivable or even feasible.

Meaningful parts of our world have, for that matter, changed so much in the last decades that for the chaos-problem, the crucial networking and feedback of sub-processes has become a factual reality. For this reason, the behavior of a system also has to be understood and described in a fundamentally differently way to the "classical" behavior of relatively more isolated (or to be treated as sufficiently isolated) single parts of a whole system.

Many areas of crisis have in the meantime made the problems of such non-linear, feedback systems obvious even to lay-people: the contamination of the water and the air, famine due to a narrow-minded foreign aid ("development aid") by Peace Corps workers trained in mechanistic science, avalanches from deforested ski mountains, as well as many other ecological catastrophes, which we experience (and further, which we initiated ourselves); national and international economic crises; the curb in the euphoria for the production power of medical-technology, etc. These phenomena and events verify drastically that the cause-and-effect model—up to now apparently so successful—has less and less grip on our modern world. It is a world whose sub-areas are so connected to one another by technological (also: communications technological) possibilities, that the effect of changes often doesn't remain locally limited. The well-meant interventions for the correction of an apparently "bad state" at one point can often lead to a break-out of its effect through the network, giving rise to highly incalculable results.

In order to understand this loss of predictability and the ability to intervene, we must take a deeper look at the phenomenon of chaos—within this scope sure enough a rather short look.

c) Deterministic Chaos

The—more precise—term "deterministic chaos" is taken to mean the phenomenon that even the simplest operations in the proper field of mathematics produce results which are, in principle, incalculable under given conditions. It is not, as we have seen, a matter of negligible questions of "accuracy". Rather, it is a matter of a fundamental problem, typical for the class of non-linear feedback systems, which an arbitrarily large accuracy also can't remedy.

Lorenz' equations were already simple. However, we can illustrate the difficulty by considering an even simpler example. For this purpose, we choose the following dynamic, which should also be understandable for those who are at loggerheads with mathematics:

$$X_{new} = (3.9 - 0.05X_{old})X_{old}$$

For the first X_{old} we can begin with a very simple value, for example 10, in order to calculate the right hand side of the equation – therefore: $(3.9 - 0.05*10)*10$, and we get $X_{new} = 34$. In the next step, this value is used again as X_{old} on the right hand side – therefore: (3.9 – 0.05*34) *34, which now gives 74.8. This procedure, in which the result of an operation serves as the initial value for the next step, is called recursion or iteration. Continuing with the iteration process for, say 50 steps, we obtain a result made up of 50 values:

Step 1: (3.9 - 0.05*10)*10   →   34
Step 2: (3.9 - 0.05*26)*34   →   74.8
Step 3: (3.9 - 0.05*46.8)*74.8 →   11.968
Step 4:   ....   →   39.51353055
....
Step 50:   ? ? ?

It is easy to calculate the steps with a pocket calculator or a PC. Actually, this ease is deceptive: The "result" of the last operation won't be correct—and it's not only an "approximation" error. Rather, different calculators or PCs (or different programs running on the same PC) will reach completely different "results". For example, it has been shown (cf. Kriz 1992, p.34) that calculations with five different computer programs produce numbers between 27.98... and 67.41... (with a possible range between 0 and 78). Nobody knows which calculation is the correct result or, at least, nearest to the correct one.

For those who are not familiar with chaos theory, this effect is totally surprising, as well as being rather easy to understand. If we multiply out the above bracketed statement, we get among other things a square (therefore: "non-linear"). A number with 2 places of accuracy needs at least 3 places when squared, one with 3 places needs at least 5, one with 5 at least 9, and so on and so forth. After 10-12 steps, we consequently need over 1000 places; after a further 10-12 steps, 1 million; then 1 billion; and our sequence of 50 steps demands, at the very least, many billions of places of accuracy—but that is beyond any computer in the world!

Already, the tiniest inaccuracy or rounding error builds itself up in subsequent calculations so much that two arbitrarily close numbers are quickly produced by very different sequences. Hence, this explains the different "results" from different computer programs which calculate the same formula in different ways. Similarly, different calculator brands come to totally different results due to their difference in design, which, for example, round the 16 places after the decimal point differently.

What we, in the abstraction of mathematics, called "no billions place accuracy", refers in reality to the fact that we just cannot measure with infinite exactness. Then, however, infinitesimal inaccuracy is enough to come to another (and once again: a completely different) course of development. And the same is true for infinitesimal influences. In the more popular discussions of chaos, this is referred to as the so-called "Butterfly Effect". According to this metaphor, the flapping of a butterfly's wings in China determines whether fine weather or a brewing hurricane will be seen over the Atlantic a month later (which shows that this metaphor refers to the starting discipline of modern chaos theory: meteorology. And, indeed, it was Lorenz who coined the term "butterfly effect".). What is meant here is that such developments have an extreme dependence on the smallest effects, flaws, modified boundary conditions, etc.

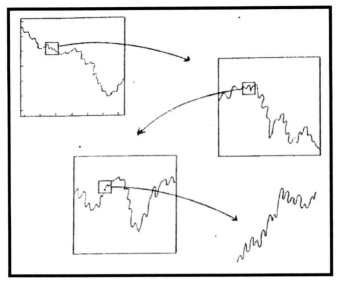

Figure 4.3. Contrary to the classical idea of the linearity of an arbitrary part of a curve, with more exact observation (or mathematical enlargements) of sufficiently small sections, fractal curves display continually more complicated characteristics.

In contrast to Figure 4.1, such curves are now characterized so that one doesn't come to linearity any more through the ever smaller, or more accurate, sections. Instead, as is shown in Figure 4.3, such sections display more and more new "complexities". It should be clear that we can say "goodbye" to planning, prediction, and diagnosis when confronted with such developments.

d) Structure—the Other Side of the Dynamics Coin

The account of the problems shown is true—but it's not the "whole truth". If it was, at this point scientists and practitioners would be better off to give up their jobs, since those processes which we deal with in our profession every day are certainly no simpler or less networked than those described above.

The "whole truth" of systems theory is much more complicated, but also more comforting for us. With "chaos theory", only one side of the interrelationship between chaos and structure in the behavior of such a dynamical system is explored. The other side is order, i.e. the same dynamics can also lead to a high stability, and both sides have to be understood in a dialectic manner.

Amazingly, this can likewise be demonstrated by means of the type of equation mentioned earlier. In this case, we reduce the first number from 3.9 to 2.2, so:

instead of $X_{new} = (3.9 - 0.05X_{old})X_{old}$,

we now have $X_{new} = (2.2 - 0.05X_{old})X_{old}$

If we again begin with 10, the sequence runs as follows:

$$X_{old} = 10$$
Step 1: (2.2 - 0.05*10)*10   → 17
Step 2: (2.2 - 0.05*17)*17   → 22.95
Step 3: (2.2 - 0.05*22.95)*22.95   → 24.15488
....

After 50 steps, we now get (on every computer, and with every program) the result: 24, 24, 24, 24, ... , i.e., we can already see after a couple of steps that the numbers converge to one value—in our case, 24. If we had chosen 2.6 instead of 2.2, this number would be 32; but if we'd chosen 3.1, for example, instead of 2.2, this would have resulted in a series that ultimately oscillates between two values, lying at approximately 34.6 and 47.4.

Quite in opposition to the earlier result, you can declare the results of not only the 50th cycle, but also of the

100th, 1000th, or millionth. Even more: now you can even miscalculate in between, make mistakes, or vary in some other way (e.g., instead of 10, begin with 8 or 30, or use 2.295 or 5.992 instead of 22.95 in the third step). The sequence will "correct" these mistakes in subsequent runs, and returns relatively fast to the value 24 (or to the value 32, or a cycle result of 34.6 or 47.4 respectively in the other examples above).

The same type of equation therefore produces extremely oppositional behavior in its dynamics. In the first case we find a high sensitivity to fluctuations in the starting values or to runtime errors from which the virtual incalculability in long-term behaviour follows. In contrast, in the second case we find a great stability in the dynamical structure, which even aspires to reach the final structure (in the simples case a number) when there are disturbances (provided that they aren't too big). Such a final structure is, incidentally, called an attractor.

e) Attractors

In order to understand this important concept a little more closely, one must first once again remember that in the cases of both chaos and order, an operation is repeatedly carried out, with the output of one iteration used as the input for the next one. This is schematically illustrated in Figure 4.4.

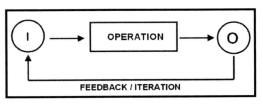

Figure 4.4: see text

This principle can be demonstrated with a simple geometrical operation. Verbally formulated, Figure 4.5 reads: "remove the middle third from a section and replace it with two thirds".[4] Carrying out this operation repeatedly on its result yields an extremely complicated shape—called a "fractal"—whose interesting properties won't however be described further here (a more exact description can be found in Kriz 1992, 1998).

For non-mathematicians, this shape is little awe-inspiring (although mathematicians called it a "monster" which undermined the entire foundations of the classical conception of "dimensionality"—which can't be described further here, cf. Kriz 1992). The next images in Figure 4.6, are, in contrast, surely more astonishing to non-experts—especially when one takes into account that these images are each based on only one operation, each one exactly as simple as that of Figure 4.5. All images begin with one section, and then only one operation is repeatedly carried out—the output of one iteration being the input for the next one.

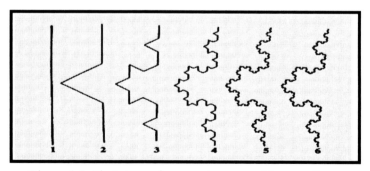

Figure 4.5: First steps of a recursive geometric operation

---

[4] Of course, other definitions are possible – for example: "replace it with a vertex of 60°"

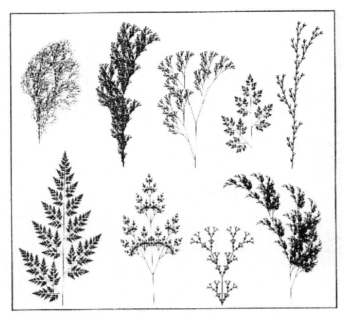

Figure 4.6. The results of some very simple recursive operations (from Kriz 1992).

Although this is not the place to go into the most profound meanings that can be associated with such pictures, it should at least be mentioned that they don't just coincidentally remind us of forms found in nature. When one points out that all forms in the living world have emerged evolutionarily as adequately stable structures in the iterative process "children of children of children of...", one gets a sense of the significance of such recursive operations for real processes.

It should be noted that it is not only the fields of physics, engineering or chemistry that are increasingly employing the dynamical systems approach. In recent times, biology and medicine have also analysed dynamics under the aspect of non-linear systems—e.g., the progressive form of a disease. In doing so, significant increases in understanding, and in the reconstruction of such progressions, have been reached.

At the same time, a particularly interesting question has not been easy to answer: How much are the processes we want to describe determined by chaotic dynamics and therefore characterized by unpredictability, and how much are they characterised by attractor dynamics and, therefore, by stability? Certain illnesses are, for example, associated with "too much order"—for instance the EEG during an epileptic fit, or certain medical parameters in osteoporosis (a disease of bone metabolism). Others, in contrast, are connected with "too little order"—for example, Cholesterolosis (a disease of the liver, more specifically of the gall bladder), or also in the case of some carcinoma (cf. Gerok 1990, Kriz 1999).

Another matter that cannot be discussed here are those interesting processes in which both aspects—chaotic and attractive dynamics—are found. These so-called chaotic attractors show continually further creative development in certain aspects (more formally: dimensions). On other dimensions, in contrast, they continuously stabilise any deviating developments. This whole complex dynamics with both unfolding and reducing tendencies reminds us of developmental processes in life, learning, organization etc. However, a description of all these interesting phenomena is beyond the scope of our discussion in this context here. At the same time, it should at least be made clear that this approach to understanding many processes in our world has been successful in many areas.

f) Cognitive and Interactive Attractors

Recalling once more what was mentioned above about the forms of living entities in our real world—namely that they have stabilised in an evolutionary process by the

recursive operation "children of children of children of..."
It is then plausible that much of what we encounter regarding long-term processes has already evolved as relatively stable attractors. Processes which are in no way stable simply cannot be cognitively grasped, described or characterised with concepts. In other words: from this perspective evolution wrenched life away from chaos (cf. Kriz 1997, 1999). This also applies to human life in particular, and to the relevant cognitive and social patterns that underlie our Lebenswelt.

The Gestalt psychologists of the 1920s and 30s, for example, have already impressively shown in numerous research publications that human perception is, to a high degree, an attractive process where the "Gestalt" is the attractor. They investigated the principles from which the order in cognitive processes arises. Besides the manifold Gestalt laws, the tendency towards Prägnanz (good form) is, in particular, widely known. Less well known is that the research in the context of this tendency towards Prägnanz had already been applied to those iterative operations which are now examined in many disciplines with regard to current discussions about chaos and structure. Such research was carried out by the British psychologist F. Bartlett in the 1930s.

One of the classical Bartlett experiments was similar to what, in a modified form, is playfully called "Chinese whispers": a person takes a piece of complex information, e.g. a long sentence, whispers it in his neighbour's ear, who then whispers what she has understood into her neighbour's ear, and so on. It is therefore a matter of a serial reproduction of (in this case) something that was heard. As is generally known, strange statements can often arise from this funny procedure.

Bartlett investigated the serial reproduction of stories in a precise way. His question was, on the one hand, which aspects of a complex story would change with serial reproduction, and on the other hand, if the content would sufficiently stabilise at some point. Without going into details, it is obvious that stories in a serial reproduction are simplified and reduced to well-ordered forms which are suited to everyday life. One is much more able, of course, to memorise and retell such simple, reduced, and consistently constructed emerging stories. Therefore the changes become smaller and smaller, and the new emerged story becomes stable in this process (cf. Bartlett 1932). As an aside, it should be noted that with this research, Bartlett was a forerunner of Jean Piaget's Schema Theory[5], which is also significant for Cognitive Psychology.

The formation of stable patterns in cognitive processes naturally holds not only for the reproduction of stories. An impressive example of the tendency towards Prägnanz by using serial reproduction in the area of visual perception is given in Figure 4.7. A complex random pattern of dots (upper left in Figure 4.7) is shown to a person as an initial stimulus for some seconds. The reproduced pattern (second pattern in the first line of Figure 4.7) is then used as the initial stimulus for the next person, and so forth. This serial reproduction procedure (or so-called Bartlett-scenario) tends to highly ordered dot patterns. The result is fascinating and simple at the same time: due to its complexity, the initial pattern cannot be memorized perfectly. It is altered during the procedure until it is so simple and well-formed that it can easily be reproduced perfectly. There is no possibility to predict what kind of pattern will be reached as an attractor. However, one can predict that it will be well-formed and simple—for example, a diamond, a cross, etc. (cf. Stadler & Kruse 1990).

---

[5] Indeed, Bartlett coined the term „Schema Theory" which was later – together with fundamental principles described by Bartlett – adopted by the famous French researcher in developmental and cognitive psychology, Piaget

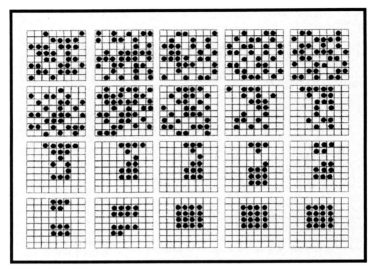

Figure 4.7. The serial reproduction of a complex point pattern using 19 successive subjects (from Stadler & Kruse 1990).

In some of the work I have initiated (see Kriz 2001 for an overview), it could be shown that such attractor dynamics are also verifiable for other cognitive processes, again by using serial reproduction. In processes of perceiving or thinking, attractor dynamics evolve, which meaningfully reduce a situation, and at the same time stabilise this reduced arrangement—analogously to the above example with the numerical attractors, or to the plant-like pictures in Figure 4.6. I have therefore coined the term "meaning-attractor", which conceptualizes these dynamic phenomena.

In addition, these results were used to make predictions about the emergence and stabilisation of patterns of interaction. Although these predictions are yet to be verified and demonstrated in detail in the laboratory, their empirical existence and relevance within the scope of systematic family and couple therapy is, however, undisputed. It is clear then that a specific cognitive diges-tion of sensual impressions to meaningful perceptions due to meaning-attractors is also a basis for specific sty-les and schemas of expression. These expressions can, accordingly, be "understood" from a communication partner using his own meaning-attractors. Therefore, iterative processes are also found in the interactions on the level of couple- and family dynamics. These allow patterns of interaction to emerge—as attractors of the interaction dynamics (referred to in the literature as, for example, "family rules"). These patterns of interaction stabilise the individual meaning-attractors on the one hand, and on the other hand are, as a result, stabilised by these sense-attractors. This is a typical circular dynamic between the macro level (patterns of interaction) and the micro level (interactions as the individual's expressions, which again can be understood to have been shaped by meaning-attractors)

Again, we cannot go into more details here. It can, however, be said in summary that our human brain is—cognitively—a generator of attractive dynamics, and that these cognitive schemas also play a central role with re-gard to the formation and stabilisation of interaction pat-terns.

The Re-Enchantment

As we have already seen at the end of the first section, the relatively long-standing and successful program of the disenchantment of the world, as carried out by occi-dental science in the 20th century—particularly in the last decades—seems increasingly questionable. Essential fun-damental assumptions of the classical world-view have proven to be false, or at the very least to be no more than special cases of a very much broader conception. Quantum mechanics has already shown that nature only makes leaps and, moreover, that our cognitive processes are much more narrowly connected with the way in which we encounter nature than was postulated by Cartesian dualism. Werner Heisenberg, the winner of the Nobel Prize for Physics, said this most aptly in a striking statement: "When we talk nowadays about the world-view of the exact natural sciences, we no longer refer to a picture of nature, but to a picture of our relationship to nature"

Chaos theory—or better and more generally: the theory of non-linear systems—has, however, changed our conception of the world even more strongly. The fundamental computability of a world understood as clockwork, a world with homogeneous parts, had to be revised to a conception in which unpredictability, qualitative leaps, big changes as a result of the smallest "causes", and dynamics with "outstanding" states (attractors) play an important and meaningful role. Moreover, for large areas of nature, these phenomena are indeed more likely to describe the normal case. At the same time, standing in contrast to this are the mechanistic principles of technology, from which chaos has been banished in order to control everything, and which have turned out to be a special artificial area of our world.

If we take these aspects seriously, then we must take certain principles into account which were been formulated by the Gestalt psychologist a hundred years ago. For example, forty years ago Wolfgang Metzger summarized "the six characteristics of working with living beings" which also formed the fundamental principles of the Humanistic Psychology of that time. Remarkably, these characteristics—earlier discredited by opponents as "lyrical" and "too unscientific"—correspond very well to the principles of modern scientific systems theory as it is described today. Without going into details, this correspondence is described by means of a comparison (see Table 1), which is discussed more thoroughly elsewhere (Kriz 1998). Nevertheless, Table 1 gives an impression of how the world reclaims a bit of the enchantment that was taken from it by classical science.

Humanistic Psychology "Six characteristics of working with living beings" (*after Wofgang Metzer 1962*)	*Modern Natural Science* Core principles of interdisciplinary systems theory
1. Non-arbitrariness of Form: One can't impose anything on the living being in the long run that is against its nature, one can only bring to development that which is already inside the "material" itself as a possibility.	One can't impose just any arbitrary form on a system; rather one can only support the organisation dynamics which are inherent to the system.
2. Formation and creation from inner power The power and drives, which actualize the forms, fundamentally have their origin in the living being one cares for.	The decisive variables of order – the so-called order parameters – essentially have their origin in the system itself.
3. Non-arbitrariness of working time The living being can not arbitrarily wait for support and nurture. It mainly has its own fruitful periods and moments for change.	Systems have a "history", relative to which "the same" interventions sometimes have no effects; however in other phases qualitative jumps can be caused.
4. Non-arbitrariness of the speed of work The processes of growth, maturity, survival of an illness, etc., evidently have their own specific speeds of development.	Phase transitions – which are perceived from outside of the system as significant qualitative changes in the dynamic structure – have system inherent ("specific") progressions.
5. The tolerance of detours One must accept detours everywhere.	The paths of development must be respected (e.g., a path through a bifurcation cannot be "shortened")

6. The reciprocity of events	Systems are not only character-
6. The reciprocity of events Events are reciprocal. In the most impressive cases, it is an encounter of "partners of life".	Systems are not only characterized by the reciprocal connections of the "elements" or sub-dynamics but the division into system and environment is purely analytic-formal. Every separation and exclusion of holistic interaction is a simplification (which may be necessary, when/if required).

Tab.4.1: Correspondence between principles of Gestalt and Humanistic Psychology and of modern interdisciplinary systems theory

We could stop here, and leave it at this message. But one would then wonder why, in spite of these insights, it is so difficult to establish these principles in the scientific community. And, even more so, why the relationships between people—in couples, families, and organisations, and also to themselves—are so often referred to as "petrified", "frozen", "hardened", and "fossilised" by psychotherapists. These descriptions refer to experiences which people suffer from as victims, although they are often enough involved as perpetrators too.

In order to understand these pathological processes, it seems to be important to again direct our attention to the significance of the sense-attractors. In the following short outline (elaborated further in Kriz 1997 and 2004), many of the aspects mentioned above will once again be illuminated from a rather phenomenological perspective. The question of how we shape and structure our Lebenswelt will also be addressed—and with this, how the tendencies to disenchantment and re-enchantment wrestle with each other and must, therefore, be balanced.

With respect to the threat posed by chaotic randomness to human experience illustrated at the beginning, it was clear that order must first be wrestled from chaos. Asking how this is done—and what the price for this order is—first involves a consideration of phylogenesis: The program of life includes namely those regularities which were found or invented in the infinite complexity of a dynamic world.

The discovery and invention of regularities is substantially based on the extreme reduction of the infinite complex process. This reduction filters only some variables out of the complexity. If, for example, very simple organisms reduce the world process only onto the variable "light", then—originating from the fact that light goes on, and after some time goes off again—categories somewhat like "morning" and "evening" arise, and with this the basis for a regularity. To be exact, no "morning" in the history of the universe was ever completely identical to another, and no "evening" was ever really identical with another. But, as far as the incomparable uniqueness of mornings can be reduced to the "reappearance of light", precisely all mornings are equal to each other (one speaks therefore of "classes of phenomenological equivalence").

For human beings, evolutionary programs of chaos avoidance have developed before language, concepts and terms emerged. Gestalt psychology, for example, has worked out how strongly our experience of the world is actively organised even at the lowest perceptual level. Perceiving means that "stimuli" are structured into "shapes". This can be demonstrated experientially, too: Points on paper are "automatically" ordered into patterns and pictures, a sequence of tones is perceived (whenever possible) as a "melody". Moreover, the constituent parts (points or tones) often obtain a new and specific meaning within these orderings. In a melody, for example, you find the phenomena of the root and the tonic keynote. Other experiments, in many variants, have demonstrated the invention of more complex ordering structures. For example, moving geometrical figures can, under certain conditions, evoke the compelling impression that they display "cause-and-effect relationships" or typical "social relationships".

However, for human beings it is significant that they can go beyond these evolutionarily and biologically acquired rules to adapt them individually and socially, and even to invent entirely new areas of rules. These are particularly useful in the individual's adaptation to his or her personal living conditions, in a more narrow sense.

Establishing order is therefore extremely necessary, for it wards off the unfathomable distress that we would otherwise fall prey to in our experiential chaos. Psychotic breakdowns and nightmares give us some insight, at an easy preliminary level, into how a world without that cognitive order would be for us. For this reason we should appreciate this positive aspect of order. The reduction of a complex, unique process to recurring classes of phenomena gives structure to chaos, makes predictions possible, and reduces insecurity; thus creating reliability. And this reliable order is with us from the first days of our life.

A typical example of this joint imparting of order and trust are the lullabies sung all over the world. They are the embodiment of regularity. Namely, they feature typically simple recurring sequences of tones. Some lullabies sing of the rising moon, the starry stars, and the reappearance of the sun. These are, evidently, the recurring and predictable aspects of a child's world. That every song is a world premiere—unique, something that has never exactly occurred before and which can never be repeated, just like every evening and every morning and like everything in our lives—this particular aspect plays no role at all. In contrast, we abstract that which the phenomena have in common, that which is similar, or in other words, familiar. Everything is then so safe, so familiar, that one no longer needs to listen and to pay attention carefully and can, like the child, doze off.

However, this establishment of intimacy and familiarity which gives us safety can be something quite dangerous in other situations. When we barely notice the details of a conversation but look for well known aspects and then respond, to ourselves or out loud, with "Oh, I already know that!"; if we already tune out after the third word, pursuing our own thoughts and not listening to what is new, then trouble is often pre-programmed. Who isn't familiar with the accusatory cry of "Hey! You're not listening to me at all!", or: "You're not listening to me properly!"?

And so we see the other side of the coin of order: at the same time, the reduction to over-familiarity closes our view to the uniqueness of the life process. And contrary to the situation in which trust and safety is confirmed by the lullaby, our conversational partner, and other people in many situations, attach importance to the fact that their words are something like a "world premiere". When we do not get involved in this dialogue, there is an exchange of flowery phrases; the unwinding of a frozen ritual, instead of an encounter. For our partner then feels, rightfully so, that he or she is not being perceived as a person but misused as an easily replaceable object whose only purpose is to set our own schemata (i.e. cognitive patterns) in motion.

The fact that everyone knows such a situation quite well shows how active this mechanism is that lets us scan the world of experience, mainly for regularities. As a matter of fact, the very same process that achieves order and safety—namely the reduction of unique situations to familiar categories—is also the gravedigger for creativity and change. And this is where unnecessary, compulsive order can set in.

As therapists, we find this impoverishment of experience in many of the people who sit facing us. But who among us can claim that he himself does not react similarly, at least to a degree, or even possibly much too strongly and much too often?

A human being does not, of course, find his particular position in the field of conflict between these two poles of "chaos" and "order" all by himself. Rather, as already pointed out earlier, the interpretations of meaning and the interaction structures of society exert a considerable influence. In particular, the occidental culture has a strong tendency to order, to reduction, and to the reification of processes.

The disenchantment of the world, which confronts us most notably as an ideology of order and control and as the illusion and mania of feasibility, has indeed been reduced ad absurdum by recent developments in science. However, the mechanistic metaphors are still having a strong influence. Without wanting to devaluate the advances and achievements of the classical scientific ideology, it must nevertheless be asserted that these metaphors and principles of explanation and understanding all too often don't meet the demands of our complex, interconnected life. The view of the world developed by modern interdisciplinary systems theory emphasises the creative aspect of chaos, and gives space to the unique aspects of the world, to intrinsic values, and to surprising novelties. In addition, this world view could contribute to a fair-living attitude in people's relationships to the world, to each other, and to themselves. It would therefore be good, if the re-enchantment of the world by modern science would affect our everyday lives and our lives in society even more strongly.

Readers are more than welcome to take these remarks as an invitation to make a contribution to the development of the re-enchantment!

References

Bartlett, F.C. (1932): Remembering. Cambridge: Cambridge Univ. Press.

Cramer, F. (1988). Chaos und Ordnung. Die komplexe Struktur des Lebendigen. Stuttgart: DVA

Gerok, W. (1990): Ordnung und Chaos in der unbelebten und belebten Natur. Stuttgart: Hirzel

Kriz, J. (1985): Grundkonzepte der Psychotherapie. Eine Einführung. München: Urban & Schwarzenberg (ab 4.Aufl. 1993: Weinheim: Psychologie Verlags Union/Beltz)

Kriz, J. (1992): Chaos und Struktur. Grundkonzepte der Systemtheorie Bd.1. München: Quintessenz

Kriz, J. (1997): Chaos, Angst und Ordnung. Wie wir unsere Lebenswelt gestalten. Göttingen: Vandenheock & Ruprecht

Kriz, J. (1998): Die Effektivität des Menschlichen . Argumente aus einer systemischen Perspektive. Gestalt Theory, 20, 131-142

Kriz, J. (1999): Systemtheorie für Psychotherapeuten, Psychologen und Mediziner. Eine Einführung. UTB/Facultas (als 3. Auflage von: Systemtheorie. Eine Einführung für Psychotherapeuten, Psychologen und Mediziner. Wien: Facultas).

Kriz, J. (2001):Self-Organization of Cognitive and Interactional Processes. In: Matthies, M, Malchow, H. & Kriz, J (Eds): Integrative Systems Approaches to Natural and Social Dynamics. Heidelberg: Springer, 517-537

Maslow, A. H. (1966): The Psychology of Science. New York: Harper & Row

Metzger, W.(1962): Schöpferische Freiheit. Frankfurt: Waldemar Kramer

Peitgen, H.-O. & Richter, P.H. (1985): The Beauty of Fractals. Berlin: Springer

Peitgen, H.-O. et. al. (1992): Chaos and Fractals. New York: Springer

Stadler, M. & Kruse, P. (1990): The Self-Organisation Perspective in Cognition Research: Historical Remarks and New Experimental Approaches. In: Haken, H. & Stadler, M. (Eds.), Synergetics of cognition. Berlin: Springer, 32-52).

Chapter 5

INTUITION
IN THERAPEUTIC PROCESSES

In the spring of 2001 I was invited to give a keynote address at the 4th convention of a major German association of systemic and family therapists. The conference theme was "intuition" and I was asked to contribute to the aspect of how a therapist can intuitively steer the therapeutic process. However, I totally dislike the idea of steering, which reminds me too much of control and of the difficulties our Western culture in engaging in processes of intuition. This is due to its reified language, as well as its metaphors and principles taken from classical mechanistic science—which has, however, permeated and merged with our every-day world. In contrast, I wanted to show that it is much easier to adequately discuss the principles of intuition within the scope of modern systems theory. With regard to psychotherapeutic practice, the facilitation of intuition calls to a great extent for the inclusion of more imaginative approaches in psychotherapy.

According to the idea that a complex subject of discourse can only be adequately approached by a multitude of perspectives, my discussion and clarification of the term "intuition" began with some narrative texts taken from different perspectives, instead of an abstract defi-nition.

Toward an Understanding of "Intuition"

Regarding the yet-to-be-developed idea of "intuition", it seems important to me that the reader is not tempted to follow this necessarily linear sequence of words in a sim-ilarly linear way, thus arriving at a pre-shaped idea. In fact, I would appreciate it if (in a concrete application of what is yet to come) the words that are read—which can be thought of as a kind of "external voice"—act as a be-neficial environmental condition to allow for the activa-tion of the reader's "internal voice", which follows more psycho-logical, socio-logical, and holistic structures than the structures of formal logic. For this reason, I won't present the reader with a (formal) logical sequence of individual arguments. Instead, I'll use an interplay of dif-ferent perspectives in the form of five aspects, images or highlights that bring out what appears to me to be funda-mental to "intuition".

i) A relevant perspective is captured by the usual defi-nitions by "intuition". For example,

Webster's Dictionary: *"...the power or faculty of at-taining to direct knowledge or cognition without evident rational thought and inference"*, or

Funk and Wagnalls Encyclopedia: *"...The concept of intuition apparently arose from two sources: the mathe-matical idea of an axiom (a self-evident proposition that requires no proof) and the mystical idea of revelation (truth that surpasses the power of the intellect)"*, and, referring to Spinoza's philosophy:*"... intuition is the highest form of knowledge, surpassing both empirical knowledge derived from the senses and "scientific"*

*knowledge derived from reasoning on the basis of ex-
perience. Intuitive knowledge gives an individual the
comprehension of an orderly and united universe and
permits the mind to be a part of the Infinite Being."*

Other dictionaries similarly stress that something is
experienced and grasped by means of intuition which we
don't (or maybe even can't) acquire in the usual rational,
planned, deliberately intellectual way. On the contrary,
"it" comes to us, and without us being able to exactly
plan or even to describe the means of this acquisition—
for example through analytical decomposition into goal-
directed steps or operationalization. But somehow, this
"it" most certainly "exists", and serves, for example, to
differentiate an intuition from a hallucination or a mere
construction of the analytical mind. Intuition is therefore
clearly directed at events "in the world", and therefore
constitutes, or even establishes a relationship between the
one having the intuition and the world.

For C.G. Jung, intuiting is therefore (along with sens-
ing) a function of the perceptual process that is distinguished from the functions of the judging processes
(thinking and feeling). This separation is however not
made in normal linguistic use. When one says that a child
intuitively grasps a situation or—even more obviously—
that you "intuitively made the right choice", then in these
cases perception and judgment are more closely connected than they are in Jungian psychology. Likewise, one
can "behave intuitively correctly"—that is, along with the
focus on the intuitive process, the surveying and evalua-
tion of a complex situation can even be extended to behavior.

Likewise, one also often speaks of "intuition" in the
case of artistic or otherwise creative processes. At any
rate, the common and meaningful core of all these interpretations of "intuition" is a non-reductionist, non-analy-
tic, holistic cognitive process in the acquisition, in the

(mostly unconscious) processing, and, if applicable, in the resulting action or expression of a complex situation.

ii) Further light can be shed on this from another perspective. In one of his writings, only a few years before his death, the famous humanistic therapist Carl Rogers wrote:

"When I am at my best, as a group facilitator or as therapist, I discover another characteristic. I find when I am closest to my inner, intuitive self, when I am somehow in touch with the unknown in me, when perhaps I am in a slightly altered state of consciousness, then whatever I do seems to be full of healing... There is nothing I can do to force this experience... ...then I may behave in strange and impulsive ways in the relationship, ways which I cannot justify rationally, which have nothing to do with my thought process. But these strange behaviours turn out to be right, in some odd way: it seems that my inner spirit has reached out and touched the inner spirit of the other. Our relationship transcends itself and becomes a part of something larger. Profound growth and healing and energy are present....this account partakes of the mystical. Our experiences in therapy and in groups, it is clear, involve the transcendent, the indescribable, the spiritual. I am compelled to believe that I, like many others, have underestimated the importance of this mystical, spiritual dimension." (Rogers 1980, p.129).

This statement of Rogers can be connected to the notion of "meaning fields" (Kriz 2004, 2006), which stresses the point that the intrapersonal as well as the interpersonal lebenswelt is structured by field forces of meaning, which act in a bottom-up and top-down interrelationship. In a two-person-relationship—client and therapist, for example—the two individuals allow a common meaning field to emerge (bottom-up) which structures the meaning of their interaction and of the topics of their interaction in a particular way (top-down). Of course, this common meaning field which emerges from the interaction of these two people is in interference with meaning fields due to their culture, their family, and their personal ontogenetic development, especially in early childhood. However, the meaning structures of culture, families, organizations, and the socialized individual are typical for the every-day understanding of our world.

They provide the self-evident background of our every-day living, and these meaning forces reduce and transform new, unknown, exciting situations to the well-known, familiar and reassured "things" of our every-day world and every-day life. In contrast, a deep and challenging encounter in a therapeutic setting (or between two people in love) does not reduce the space of meaning to the well-known but, conversely, opens up this space to new experiences and understanding. In this moment, the "world" is less shaped by the narratives of the every-day world and every-day life—or even by the narratives of Western science—but more by an unfolding phenomenological experience of what is happening. And in order to share these experiences with the other person, in order to communicate and, therefore, to symbolize the experience, a common meaning field emerges which allows these two people to understand each other—not only from the perspective of every-day understanding, but also in a way that is somehow distinct from that every-day standpoint.

It is important to consider that—in contrast to the analytical dismantling of our experiences into the parts of a rational reconstruction of or world in the context of classical science—our phenomenological experience is much more meaningful in a holistic way.

When we ring at the downstairs door of a high building and at this very moment a flower-pot falls out of a window of the 4th floor, what we experience is that we have caused this. The second step is, of course, to question this experienced causality, to analytically dismantle the situation and decide that this description of our experience is "non-sense" (that is: makes no sense in the rationality of our Western culture) and that the "correct" description of what "really" happened is to say that we "observed" two events—ringing and a falling flower-pot—with no causal relationship other than random coincidence. Accordingly, when a triangle "attacks" a circle very quickly and strongly from the left and the circle jumps to the right on a screen or in an animated cartoon, what we experience is the leap of the circle caused by the triangle. Again, by dismantling our holistic experience, we infer the "description" that we just "interpreted" the causality.

However, that's not true: causality is what we experience, and what we interpret is that there was no "real" causality but "two stimuli, a triangle and a circle", moving in a special way. Moreover, according to the work of the Gestalt Psychologists of the Berlin School in the first decades of the 20th century, social interrelationship are also often experienced and not "interpreted"—for example, the experience that the triangle pushes the circle aggressively or, in other cases, that the triangle approaches the circle very cautiously. Of course, these causal and social meaning structures of our phenomenological experience are due to the evolution of man—and, in addition, to the evolution of society and its "cognitive enslavement" by way of socialization.

Taking this into account does not mean playing the forces of these evolutionary meaning structures off against the forces of the meaning structures due to the narratives of our every-day world or even of our scientific narratives. It is helpful to understand that the experience of cause is sometimes misleading—as it was in the case of the relationship between "ringing the bell" and "the fall of the flower pot". However, this should not be a question of right or wrong—because in most cases nobody knows what the "correct" principle of explanation is and what the wrong one is. For example, the flower pot could have been thrown down by a lady who dislikes people ringing at her door so often—and then the ringing was really an important "cause" in this situation (besides the causes in the world-view of that lady and her actions).

More specifically, what are the "correct" causes in a therapeutic process that "change" the client's understanding of himself and of his world and, as a result, changed his actions and behavior? As we know from modern science, especially from systems theory, many well-known scientific ideas and principles of explanation have turned out to be incorrect (at least with regard to the postulated generality). For instance, in some states of a system S, very small changes of X can "cause" very big effects on Y, while in other phases, the system compensates even for rather big "causes".

This is even more important in our social world, where the forces of meaning and values are often much stronger than scientifically proven facts (if such facts exist at all). My belief that I am a person beloved by my wife or my family shapes my social relationship to them and my actions much more strongly than any measurement of their "real love", as computed by a scientist. Therefore, again, instead of "right" or "wrong", it is more important to consider which principles of explanation and narratives open up the space of meaning and, as a consequence, facilitate the creativity of new ways of acting, in contrast to those principles that narrow down that space. We should be aware that in many cases the "scientific" principles (meaning the principles of a mechanistic world view) and their effects on our every-day world (due to 400 years of successful influence by mechanistic science on our culture) do not open up the space of meaning, understanding and potential acting, but instead narrow it down.

Therefore, the causal and social meaning forces in our experience are as real as the "things" in our phenomeno-logical world. To argue from a scientific perspective that there are no "real" causal or social relationships but that it is our mind which binds phenomena together is as true as stating that we cannot perceive houses, trees, or faces. We know from scientific analysis that there are only parts of such things on our retina, actively scanned by the mind (and the brain, of course) by way of short eye-movements (saccades) and then bound together by the mind into a "house", a "tree" or a "face". And it should be mentioned that it is not the "thing" itself, or the biological mechanics of our brain, but the mind which structures this process; because we know from science that the path of the eye-movements is greatly dependent on the intention (or, ex-perimentally, the given task) to find out something about the "stimulus structure". The same picture of a scene is scanned in a totally different way when we want to find out the social relationship or the age of the persons, for example (cf. Yarbus 1967).

Therefore, in accordance with Rogers' statement, our world is filled with much more complex meaning fields when we are in situations which are removed from the every-day necessities of reducing and transforming our rich experience to the well-known, familiar and reassured "things" of our every-day world and every-day life.

It is no wonder that this experience can be symbolized by referring to "mystical and spiritual dimensions" as Rogers did. When a common meaning field emerges which is beyond the reducing principles of every-day ex-planations, when "the inner spirit reaches out and touches the inner spirit of the other" as Rogers very appropriately phrased it, we need the terms "mystical" and "spiritual" to describe this experience from the perspective of every-day language—knowing that only those who have had similar experiences can adequately understand it. This is, however, true for all symbolizations of experiences. For many this description of a "mystical" and "spiritual" experience is comparable to the description of "red" to a blind person or "love" to somebody who has never known such a feeling.

Interestingly, in an article on "religion" in Funk and Wagnalls Encyclopedia there is a very meaningful correspondence to our point. First, the article reports that western civilization has (in the main) lost a type of consciousness where the internal and external worlds are much more related to each other. In many "primitive cultures" there is not such a sharp boundary between the spiritual and the natural world, and thus between the human mind or ego and the surrounding world. It continues:

"The French philosopher Lucien Levy-Bruhl (1857-1939) called this absence of boundary participation mystique ("mystical participation"), denoting a sense of fusion between the human organism and its environment. This feeling may be described as corresponding on its own level with the modern intellectual grasp of humanity's interrelationship with nature in the science of ecology.

A similar absence of boundary prevails also between the worlds of waking experience and dream, and between the individual will and the spontaneous emotions and drives of the psyche. As a result the whole external world is charged with powers that may be called mental or spiritual. Material objects, as stable and comprehensible features of the external world, do not exist, for everything seems to behave as whimsically as the events in dreams. Uncontrolled as the contents of experience may be in this state of mind, they would appear to be so lively, mysterious, and fascinating, as well as terrifying, that the whole of nature is suffused with an atmosphere of the awesome and uncanny. The German religious historian Rudolf Otto referred to such an atmosphere as the "numinous."

Otto himself stated that "the non-rational apprehension of the Holy, or "numinous," has two aspects: fascination, or attraction, and awe." When we take this into consideration, then these two aspects also describe the way Rogers encountered his clients.

Finally, another part of this article should be cited in our context:

"Basically, the numinous atmosphere is attached to the entire natural world and every object within it. A good example may be seen in Shinto, a present-day "primitive" religion practiced in the sophisticated civilization of Japan. The Japanese term shinto (Jap. shin,"spirit") means "the way of the gods" or "the way of spirit." In the view of Shinto, every rock, tree, animal, and stream has its own shin or kami (Jap., "god" or "goddess"). It is, however, misleading to call the kami a god in any Western sense of the word; similarly, the term shin means "spirit" only in an extremely vague sense, for it is used often simply as an exclamation similar to "Wonderful!" Shinto has no system of doctrine, no creed, and no formulated religious ideas; it is fundamentally concerned with expressing wonder, respect, and awe for everything that exists. This concern involves treating everything as if it were a person, not always in the sense that it is inhabited by some humanlike ghost or spirit, but in the sense of having a mysterious and independent life of its own that may not be taken for granted."

Indeed, "wonder, respect, and awe" are not the typical features in approaches that want to control everything. And "treating everything as if it were a person" is diametrically opposed to the approach of treating every person as if it were an anonymous carrier of symptoms. No wonder then that intuition or the experience Rogers described are not considered to be phenomena in today's mainstream.

iii) A third example takes this theme of looking beyond usual everyday experience to a greater extreme. A case history of the famous psychiatrist Oliver Sacks deals with a severely retarded and autistic pair of twins, who were still confined to a clinic as adults because they simply couldn't provide for themselves. They were unable to carry out simple arithmetic problems like the addition of two numbers, yet Sacks reports:

"A box of matches on their table fell, and discharged its contents on the floor: '111,' they both cried simultaneously; and then, in a murmur, John said '37'. Michael repeated this, John said it a third time and stopped.

I counted the matches - it took me some time - and there were 111. 'How could you count the matches so quickly?' I asked. 'We didn't count,' they said. 'We saw the 111.' ... 'And why did you murmur '37,' and repeat it three times?' I asked the twins. They said in unison, '37, 37, 37, 111'

And this, if possible, I found even more puzzling. That they should see 111—'111-ness'—in a flash was extraordinary ... But they had then gone on to 'factor' the number 111—without having any method, without even 'knowing' (in the ordinary way) what factors meant. Had I not already observed that they were incapable of the simplest calculations, and didn't 'understand' (or seem to understand) what multiplication or division was? Yet now they had divided a compound number into three equal parts.

'How did you work that out?' I said, rather hotly. They indicated, as best as they could, in poor, insufficient terms—but perhaps there are no words to correspond to such things—that they did not 'work it out', just but 'saw' it, in a flash." (Sacks 1990, p. 200)

After further investigation, Sacks found out that the two were in the habit of conversing with each other in prime numbers of six or more digits, even though there is no simple mathematical method of determining whether numbers of such size are prime or not. Again, the twins could give no explanation for this, other than that they would "see" these numbers.

This example raises questions about an explanation of this strange ability and about what can be "seen" at all in the case of prime numbers—in other words, what exactly do the prime numbers refer to beyond the cultural construct of mathematics (which the twins have barely mastered)? Naturally, one might appeal to the numerical mysticism of Pythagoras and Plato's "Ideals" (which, incidentally, also interested Kepler and C.G Jung in the form of "archetypes", and is still a subject of some research in the modern natural sciences—cf. Kriz 1997), but these ideas certainly can't deliver an "explanation" in the usual sense of the word.

iv) A further case study from Sacks should make it clear how a "handicap" in everyday abilities can in fact increase sensitivity, here in a situation that is more appropriately judged in an intuitive way, while we "overlook" it in our normal every-day mindset, and are thus deceived:

During a television broadcast of a speech by an American president (presumed to be Reagan), most of the patients of the hospital ward were doubled over with laughter, others appeared worried and confused, while Sacks and the rest of the staff noticed nothing special about the speech. The ward was for aphasic patients, who in the most severe cases cannot understand the meaning of words due to a disruption or injury to the sensory language centre (located in the left temporal lobe). Aphasics can nevertheless understand most of what you say to them in normal situations. They derive this meaning from the speaker's gestures, facial expressions, intonation, rhythm, melody, etc., and for that reason it follows that they are by necessity particularly sensitive. "Thus," in the detailed report of the patients' reaction to the president's speech, Sachs writes: *"it was the grimaces, the histrionisms, the false gestures and, above all, the false tones and cadences of the voice, which rang false for these wordless but immensely sensitive patients. It was to these (for them) most glaring, even grotesque, incongruities and improprieties that my aphasic patients responded, undeceived and undeceivable by words. This is why they laughed at the President's speech."*

Another patient in the ward reacted similarly, but in her case however, she suffered from total agnosia, due to damage to the right temporal lobe. To understand what was said to her, she had to depend completely on the words spoken and on their relationship to one another, as she no longer had the ability to grasp the "evocative" part of speech—the part which is conveyed by intonation and feeling, for example. When asked about the president's speech, she remarked: "His word-use is improper. Either he is brain-damaged, or he has something to conceal."

Sacks summarizes: *"We normals—aided, doubtless, by our wish to be fooled, were indeed well and truly fooled. And so cunningly was deceptive word-use combined with deceptive tone, that only the brain-damaged remained intact, undeceived".* (Sacks 1990, p. 84)

v) This sensitivity of the impaired compared to us "normals" leads directly to the last aspect I want to discuss. During the training and supervision of young therapists, I have become increasingly convinced that one of the most important abilities that I would like to help these trainees to develop is based upon this very sensitivity. It is a sensitivity for their own intuitive processes, but as we have seen, this includes at the same time a sensitivity for the holistic complexity of a situation. This sensitivity is also geared towards interactions (and here, I would even prefer to say: towards encounters) with the patient, and therefore also intuitively grasps many aspects of their expression. Again, these outward expressions are, of course, the externalization of complex inner processes.

This sounds equally as vague as demanding. Both aspects must then be relativized—and so more context should be given. Considering this development of intuitive skills as a demand in the classical way of teaching and learning can lead to the exact opposite of the desired outcome. A demand that doesn't have an obvious means of being fulfilled can lead to tension and anxiety which then obstructs the processes of intuition. What is meant here is rather openness to unconventional experiences—sensitivities, thoughts and perceptions—with a minimal amount of rash censorship or categorisation.

However, it is the traditional methods of teaching that all too often obstruct access to this sensibility. The factual and theoretical knowledge and ideas, the diagnostic and other clinical categories instead hinder any involvement with the kind of relationship that Rogers, for example, spoke of. This should not be considered as a criticism of such topics of teaching. In many contexts and situations, a professional therapist must show something quite different from this sensitivity in the therapeutic relationship. For example, he has to argue with health insurance bodies, he has to prove that he is effective and he has to write reports for the controlling systems.

On the other hand, a world view seen through the cognitive glasses of pre-defined categories is of no benefit to this therapeutic relationship, which is essential for the healing processes in humanistic therapies. And it is of no benefit to intuition. Also, it is obvious that therapists who mistrust their own intuitions and who correspondingly don't allow these intuitive processes to have an effect, instead trusting primarily in principles of external order, can hardly invite patients to explore and foster their intuitive forces and abilities.

Intermediate summary: When one summarizes what the essential aspects of the five exemplary perspectives I have chosen have to say about the meaning of "intuition", then we can see that it concerns an access to the understanding of processes that don't follow the normal, everyday, rational, planned and goal-directed path in an analytical-categorical (and thus more left hemispherical) manner. Rather, they open up events in a much more holistic (more right hemispherical) and observational-contemplative fashion. The insight occurs unintentional and suddenly—similarly to the "aha!"-effect investigated in Gestalt psychology and described as a sudden phase transition in processes of problem solving, for example. In addition, it seems appropriate here to include a reference to Martin Buber (1996), who wrote: "The You encounters me by grace—it cannot be found by seeking."

As a hypothesis, I would like to add that these sudden intuitive ideas probably grasp the manifest order of the processes to a lesser degree than the latent ordering factors or principles—that is, those structuring forces which produce order. This will be discussed in more detail later on.

Intuition in social and scientific context(s)

In the mainstream sciences (including psychology), "intuition" is a concept that has been comparatively under-researched. If anything, one can even say that Western science banished the idea of intuitive access "to the world", for example, during the battle against witchcraft

and alchemy. Instead, science gave a one-sided preference to the analytic-discursive approach. While Kepler,
for example—who still partly shared the views of the
Middle Ages—in spite of all experimental and mathematical precision, proceeded rather intuitively with his research into planetary orbits and wanted to depict the divine harmony of the cosmos, the motives of the "fathers"
of modern science, Bacon, Descartes, and Newton, were
quite different (see chapter 2).

In summary, one can say that Western science mainly
propagates a means of access to the world in which intuitive, holistic, and qualitative (in the sense of "qualia")
aspects are irrelevant. And, in contrast to the development of modern science, this access is still the leading
example for many scientists in the field of psychology
and even psychotherapy.

In the context of our problem, this would be at best an
interesting remark for the history of science if this approach to the world had limited itself to making science.
But, the development of science has influenced our culture so significantly and penetrated its bounds of common sense in such a way that these scientific maxims and
metaphors have also become the main way of thinking in
our everyday world. This is often particularly true for the
Lebenswelt of patients, who all too often try to compensate for their lack of trust in the processes of self-organization and in their sensitivity for favourable conditions
for development, by controlling their own life processes
and those of others—generally with only limited success.

Of course, this ideology also doesn't contribute to the
improvement of intuition for therapists. For example,
whenever we talk about "quality control" in psychotherapy, it almost exclusively means the goal-oriented
achievement of pre-defined, over-simplified quantitative
measures of low complexity. The efficacy of psychotherapy is operationally defined, and is therefore reduced

to whichever aspect can be empirically grasped easily and well—intuition certainly does not fit here. "Good" and "effective" therapeutic procedure is tied too much to a compliance with the rules and regulations that are prescribed in manuals. In such contexts, intuition then appears to be superfluous—at best, it is reduced here and there to aspects that can be trained, and embedded in manuals.

In contrast to the everyday opinion of the "principles of science", which to a great extent date back to the 19th Century, the research in modern systems science certainly has a lot to say about processes that are also relevant for intuition. Indeed, there are even areas of science that make use of intuition in undreamt of ways—for instance the mathematical investigation of fractal geometry. Some leading mathematicians in this area depict non-linear dynamics graphically on a computer screen, and these images can bring them to intuitive insights and hypotheses.

The derivations and proofs involved are of course still purely mathematical, but the results—which, in general, suggest the best direction for investigation and an idea of what might be significant and interesting there—are gained through visual intuition. Here, one obviously makes use of the abilities of the human cognitive apparatus (perception, attention, awareness and cognitive processing) to rapidly discover regularities in complex structures by means of visual depiction. These regularities could possibly be very weak, or maybe are yet to unfold in the continuing dynamic. In both cases, intuition is clearly superior to any mathematical-algorithmic screening method.

It is exactly this aspect which seems to me to also to be important for therapeutic intuition. Dynamics or developments, which in their early stages are not yet very distinctive, but move towards an order that becomes increasingly apparent, are quite often intuitively grasped. Using the concept of "attractor", exactly this phenomenon is investigated and discussed in systems science: In the development and change of dynamic order, a process moves towards a state of order (the attractor) that is only gradually established. Without question, this concerns a teleological principle that was banished from classical Western science a long time ago because of its "obscurity". Now, as a result of the "attractor" concept, it has returned again with dignity to modern natural science. From the perspective of established order, one can also say that a still very incomplete order becomes increasingly completed during an attracting process (the so-called "completion dynamics").

Without going into detail here (see Kriz 1992, 1999a, b), this process can be illustrated as in Fig.5.1. In this figure, an operation (or transformation) is carried out on a randomly chosen point, which then produces another point. The same operation is then carried out on this new point, and so on; and in this way increasingly many more points arise. The iterative application concerns one (or very few—here: 4) operations. According to the operation rules (equations that describe the transformations), a "fern" (Fig.5.1a), for example, or a "maple leaf" (Fig.5.1b) arise. The entire procedure can be understood as a dynamic process, out of which the form (order) of the "leaf" or "fern" increasingly develops. The images on the right each contain 10,000 points, those in the middle contain 500, and the pictures on the left have only 50 points. Nevertheless, the developing order can already be recognized in the middle image (which contains only 5% of the final number of points).

When considered in the context of the therapeutic process, the dynamic structures, rules, and orders are on the one hand cognitive structures—these are meaning and sense structures (in Osnabrueck we have introduced the term "sense attractor"), patterns in the shapes of thought and argumentation, cognitive-emotional schemata, etc. On the other hand, and connected, there are the structures of communication that are important for psychotherapy— structures in the patient-therapist-relationship and structures in couples and families (or even organizations). With respect to intuition, it is helpful to make these structures visible and open to experience. This can be done, for example, through sculpture or through psychodramatic techniques.

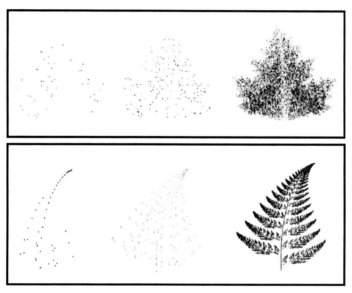

Fig. 5.1a,b : Iterative point dynamics, each based on 4 transformations (from Kriz 1992), see text for explanation.

The answer to the question of exactly what it is that is special about the dynamic principle of developing order, as compared to the classical analytic-synthetic idea of order is perhaps made even more clear in Fig. 5.2. The plant-like image on the right can be produced using the "normal" conception of order (and classical geometry) by means of a long series of instructions of the following form: "draw a straight line of x cm; then after y cm from the starting point move to the right by z degrees and draw again…" One would need very many such instructions, but in principle it is possible to use this method to produce exactly this drawing. In fact, it's possible that there are many people who might regard this as the only possibility of producing it.

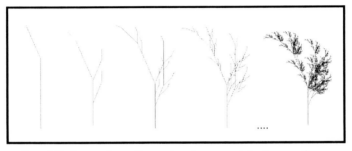

Fig. 5.2: Recursion of one simple geometrical operation

The alternative possibility is described by the sequence of pictures beginning on the left. In this case, it is a matter of only one simple operation that is carried out on the first picture on the left. The same operation is then performed on the result (second picture from left), and so on. After just six such repetitions ("recursions"), the picture on the right already appears. This process of development—which could even be called the "unfolding" of the ordering potential of this operation—is indeed very different to the step-wise linking of lines in the operation first described above. However, in the step-wise production every step can be controlled and compared to the final picture in order to detect errors and to correct them. In the dynamic of unfolding, in contrast, one has to trust that the final order will emerge, because for many iterations (or: for a long time in the process) it is not so evident that the process will really arrive at that form (especially when the forms are more complex—for example a photo of a face). And, as we already discussed, for many people (and organizations) it is much more comfortable to control than to trust.

By implementing such development processes in a computer program and using more complex end-pictures, it becomes clear that a holistic-intuitive means of access can already grasp and "anticipate" the emerging order at a rather early stage.

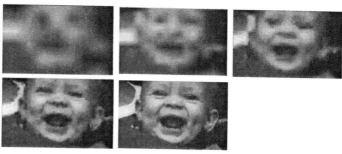

Fig.5.3: Recursion of more complex geometrical operations (but in general the same procedure of fractal encoding and decoding as in Fig.5.2)

This was shown in Fig.5.1, where a very slight development of the order—that is, a very small part of the final information—could be seen and completed intuitively to arrive at the final picture (fern or leaf). The final order—the "attractor"—exists only at the "end" of the development (given a certain time-window in which to observe the development). But the ordering forces (called "order parameters" in Synergetics) increasingly manifest the order in a way that can be discerned by a cognitive system. Subjectively, the order—that is the figure—appears "as if out of a mist". It is not a case of "clear detail" after "clear detail" that fit together into a whole. Rather, a holistic shape forms from the beginning—a shape that is, however, very unclear and blurry at first, gradually becoming clearer. This is shown in Fig.3.

From this perspective, intuition can be characterized as the ability to grasp developing or unfolding (or in some way: changing) order in its essential aspects and as a complete whole, even in the early stages of development, when this order can only later be fully described in an analytic way.

Aspects for Therapeutic Practice

In the preceding section, the scientific principles of a holistic–intuitive acquisition were discussed. It is no co-incidence that this section ended with an example from geometry—something that could be visualized in a diagram or a picture—while in the first section (in which societal opposition to a stronger consideration of intuition was highlighted) the discussion was more about language, categories, and things. In fact, terms, concepts, and categories, together with a reified language, function as very strong cognitive attractors. In contrast to attractor dynamics, which are intuitively grasped during the emergence and change of order in the "here and now", the typical cognitive attractors in our culture conservatively describe the status quo. Cognitive attractors—or "sense attractors" as we call them in our research in Osnabrück—therefore take effect in direct opposition to the emergence of new order and tendencies towards change in already established order.

A term like "behavioral disturbance"—perhaps in the context of the statement: "Young Hans has a behavioral disturbance"—operates as a reification, and is rather resistant to changes, even if it may be "intuitively" clear that the above statement can't capture the whole truth. That's why therapists who use a systems perspective— and that includes Rogers' person centered approach—try to resolve the inflexibility of ascriptions by means of a "liquefaction" of linguistic sense processes. Already the statement "Hans behaves in a disturbed way" brings up questions like: "when?" and "in which context?" that wouldn't come up before. And a deeper discussion of these questions leads to a complex structure, made up of various situations in which much of Hans' "disturbance" can be understood (e.g. as a "natural reaction" to his sister's behavior at the time), or seen in a different light (e.g. as "attention-seeking" or as a "distraction from a developing conflict between his parents", etc.). His parents might then say, "We intuitively knew that much of what Hans did meant something else." But before that insight, the attractive power of the term and concept of "behavioral disturbance" had fixed the intuitive view of the complex diversity of the situations involved and of their meaning onto this single "cause" that must "lie within Hans".

This example should serve as an illustration for the fact that language and its customary categorizations, terms, and narratives can often obstruct the intuition for seeing helpful developments. Furthermore, through language, the diversity and complexity of situations are often broken down into reductive alternatives, like good vs. evil, true vs. false, guilty vs. innocent, sick vs. healthy. Certainly, it must also be taken into consideration that without reduction and categorization we simply could not survive (Kriz 1997). And so, when considered in the strictest sense, the point is not to live without categories, rather to first liquefy established and malignant categories in order to then come to helpful sense categories and interpretations that will open up the cognitive space of options for interpretation and action.

If one agrees with this, and appropriately takes the relevance of a teleological development perspective sketched above into account, then the result is a plea for the greater consideration of imaginative courses of action for the improvement of intuitive processes.

Compared with language, imagination is rather right hemispherical, holistic and integrative. Imagination has a strong teleological character—at its core, images and ideas are created that are then transferred to or realized through action. Such imaginative procedures are, in many cases, already used in systemic therapy.

The "wonder question" in systemic therapy—"Tomorrow morning when you wake up, and X has changed, how will you notice the change?"—is one example of a typically imaginative technique. It allows playful possibilities and contrasts in developments to originate in front of the mind's eye, which will maybe only later (and mostly in a way that is still very unclear) be realized. And as is well known, these "wonder questions" are particularly effective in the interaction between therapist and client(s) when they are substantial, suggestive and persuasive, rich in detail, and attractively described with great "pulling" power.

In exactly the same way, the typically solution-oriented question of "exceptions" (in the cases of suffering, symptoms, troubling situations, etc.) is an invitation for the imagination of possible solutions, which admittedly were already present for the individual and already used by that person, but which were, however, hidden from the intuitive view by the current sense attractors (and their linguistic-semantic categories). This is, by the way, typical for attractor landscapes. The next valley in such a landscape—which could perhaps be connected with a better solution for the entire dynamic—is concealed by the hills of the landscape. First, the system must surmount these hills so it can approach a new attractor. This is not a matter of fundamentally "new" solutions, rather of solutions that were already available and which had already begun to become apparent (and this is where the question of exceptions comes into play). But such solutions must still be moved into the cognitive centre in order to unfold their effectiveness and attractiveness to change the dynamic order.

The encouragement of intuition does not mean the same for therapists and clients. In the case of therapists, it concerns an improvement in the ability to perceive unfolding developments much earlier than a rational-analytical look at the details allows. In the case of patients, it's a matter of how the development of future images, for example in the form of poetic narratives, metaphors etc., can be fostered by the therapist. If this is a success—and this needs a dignified examination of the motives that were underlying the troublesome images so far—such images can develop an almost magical attractive force. The therapist, together with the patient, then develops a space for unfolding potentials—a kind of "play space"— in which intuition is playfully, artistically, and creatively given space in order to develop helpful ideas through imagination.

Here, "future image" shouldn't be understood so much in the everyday sense, for instance "imagining a picture of the future". Rather, it is also a matter of an intuitive reference to aspects of one's own experience that are already there and have been sensed to some extent, but are still unclear. These aspects manifest themselves during the therapeutic process with increasing clarity over time, and, in addition, they also extensively symbolize. Because it is an integral part of human nature to come into contact with oneself, experiencing and exploring one's inner aspects, and in doing so, to come to an increasing understanding of oneself by symbolizing the intuitively felt meanings of one's own life processes (an aspect that is central to the therapist's work, especially in the person-centered approach, or in "focusing"—cf. Gendlin 1998).

In principle, these intuitive and imaginative processes are admittedly more difficult to accompany by means of language—due to the above-mentioned tendencies towards reification, polarization, static-logic thought structures (as opposed to dynamic-fluid "fuzzy sets"), reductionist claims of truth, etc.—than for example with the help of techniques from the "expressive arts" (Kriz 1999b). There is a lot of evidence and much research has been carried out—especially by Julius Kuhl and his group in Osnabrück (cf. Kuhl 2001)—which shows that activation of the right hemisphere, more specifically of the right frontal lobe, supports the function of the "extension memory", which is a system providing implicit representations of extended semantic networks, specialized in parallel-holistic and poly-semantic information processing. According to Kuhl's PSI theory (Personality Systems Interactions), which itself integrates a lot of research and findings of others, the activation of these extended associative networks may be regarded as the functional basis of intuitive judgements. The parallel-distributed processors are capable of handling vast amounts of complex information at speeds that greatly exceed the capacity of the conscious mind. And these parallel-holistic, poly-semantic, and integrative processing characteristics make the right hemisphere especially suited for processing integrated self-aspects or self-images (cf. Baumann, Kuhl & Kazén, 2006).

The left hemisphere, in contrast, is specialized in analytical, sequential and "monosemantic" (i.e., unambiguous) information processing. According to PSI-theory, a system called "intention memory" (Kuhl & Kazén, 1999) is specialized in the analytical-sequential processing of verbal information and explicitly formulated goals. Activation of this system may help to maintain the cognitive representation of intentions, but it may not necessarily help in checking the self-compatibility of goals. Baumann, Kuhl & Kazén (2006) additionally point out that in order to make progress on a planned action, cognitive processing has to be reduced to information that is relevant for the imminent action.

A lot of research on PSI theory shows that the activation of right-hemispheric processing is related to mental health and well-being—for instance protects persons from falsely attributing assigned goals as being self-selected in memory, and facilitates self-integration; while, on the contrary, a deficit in right-hemispheric functioning is associated with several pathological processes. For example, Weinberg (2000) has proposed that the production of a shift to left-hemispheric functioning is involved in the pathology of suicidal persons, which includes disintegration of self-representations, overly general nature of personal memories, and alienated and negative perception of the body.

In our context, it is important that activating the right hemisphere—and hence facilitating self-integration—can be done by focusing the cognitive activities on holistic, intuitive-creative activities as well as by body-sensing. Although these findings should be discussed in much more detail—for example, the relationship of these processes to personality dispositions (cf. Kuhl 2001)—it is remarkable how much they are in agreement with our discussion of sequential, verbal, categorical versus holistic, dynamical, intuitive processes.

However, left-hemispherical language can most certainly be used to initiate and support right-hemispherical processes. As well as in the case of the use of artistic language (poetry, metaphors, etc.), this already happens in verbal instructions for the furthering of non-verbal processing aspects, for example, expressing relationships in a family by making a "sculpture" of the family members. It is not the use of language per se that is important, rather the way in which it is used.

For example, if with these thoughts poured into language, I have managed to succeed in awakening ideas about possible small changes in the reader's work methods or in the reconstruction of these methods, then the purpose of this contribution has been fulfilled.

References

Baumann, N. Kuhl, J. & Kazén, M. (2006): Left-Hemispheric Activation and Self-Infiltration: Testing a Neuropsychological Model of Internalization Motivation and Emotion (i.pr.)

Buber, M. (1996) I and Thou. (A new translation by Walter Kaufmann), New York: Simon & Schuster

Gendlin, E.T. (1998) Focusing. Reinbek b. Hamburg: Rowohlt

Kriz, J. (1992) Chaos und Struktur. Systemtheorie Bd 1. München, Berlin: Quintessenz

Kriz, J. (1997): Chaos, Angst und Ordnung. Göttingen/Zürich: Vandenheock & Ruprecht

Kriz, Jürgen (1999a): Systemtheorie für Psychotherapeuten, Psychologen und Mediziner. Wien: Facultas/UTB (3rd ed.)

Kriz, J. (1999b): On Attractors - The Teleological Principle in Systems Theory, the Arts and Therapy. POIESIS. A Journal of the Arts and Communication, 24-29

Kuhl, J. (2001): Motivation und Persönlichkeit. Interaktionen psychischer Systeme. Göttingen: Hogrefe

Kuhl, J. & Kazén, M. (1999). Volitional facilitation of difficult intentions: Joint activation of intention memory and positive affect removes stroop interference. Journal of Experimental Psychology: General, 128, 382-399

Rogers, C.R. (1980) A Way of Being. New York: Houghton Mifflin

Rogers, C.R. (1986) Ein klientenzentrierter bzw. personzentrierter Ansatz in der Psychotherapie. In Rogers, C. R. & Schmid, P.F. 1991: Person-zentriert. Mainz: Matthias Grünewald, 238-256)

Sacks, O. (1990): The Man who Mistook His Wife for a Hat. New York: HarperCollins

Sparrer, Insa & Varga von Kibéd, Matthias (2000): Ganz im Gegenteil. Tetralemmaarbeit und andere Grundformen systemischer Strukturaufstellungen – für Querdenker und solche, die es werden wollen. Heidelber: Carl-Auer-Systeme (2nd ed.).

Weinberg, I. (2000). The prisoners of despair: Right hemisphere deficiency and suicide. Neuroscience and Biobehavioral Reviews, 24, 799-815.

Yarbus, A.(1967) Eye Movement and Vision. New York: Plenum Press

Chapter **6**

(SELF)-ACTUALIZATION
MEANING STRUCTURES AND
MEANING FIELDS

This chapter is composed of extracts from different papers written (and mostly published in German) during the last years. The leitmotif was to work out the (self-) actualization of meaning in an interactive context – such as the client-therapist relationship. From my point of view, the underlying theory (the „Person-centered Systems Theory") could serve very well to provide a deeper understanding of this problem because of its multi-level conception, which explicitly considers the interwoven top-down and bottom-up perspectives of complex processes. The conception of fields in particular is just as interesting as it is fundamental for the understanding of some processes involved in an encounter. Meaning fields, structured by order parameters, emerge in a bottom-up fashion from the dynamic of the parts (here: individual interpretations, aspects of understanding, and meaning), while they simultaneously influence and shape the dynamic of these parts in a top-down way. Although a few concepts of systems theory do require further clarified a little more, I tried to keep the text as simple, illustrative, and vivid as possible.

The Meaning Structures of our Lebenswelt: Necessary and Dangerous.

The human Lebenswelt is meaningful and filled with sense. This is because living as a human means finding sense in the world, in the actions of other people, and in one's own expressions of life. As social creatures, humans share this world with others by communicating. What's more, living as a human involves situating oneself "in the present" on the time-line of past–present–future, and placing one's own framework for living in the context of this sense and temporality.

Whatever we do—we can't do otherwise—we interpret and decipher the experiences we have in our life processses in our encounters with the world, with other people, and ultimately with ourselves, and embed these experiences in the meaning structures of our Lebenswelt. This doesn't just apply to the everyday world; it is even true in the context of scientific enquiry—it is only through sense-based encounters that we can find out something about the world, as the physicist Werner Heisenberg emphasized so aptly almost half a century ago. "Natural science does not simply describe and explain nature," said Heisenberg in Physics and Philosophy (1958), "it is a part of the interplay between nature and ourselves; it describes nature as exposed to our method of questioning."

Relationships and encounters are always both *impressive* and *expressive*. People's impressions and expressions are dynamically inter-related to one another. This dynamic connection between impressive and expressive vitality is dealt with, for example, in ideas like the *Merkwelt*[1] and

---

[1] the set of all environmental factors that are significant for a species, whether or not they are actually perceptible. *Merkwelt* is a species'

Wirkwelt[2] (operational world) of J. v. Uexküll's (1920) "functional cycles" or V. v. Weizsäcker's (1940) "Gestaltkreis"[3]. In the understanding of today's natural sciences, we get nothing more and nothing less from nature than a specific answer to each of our specific questions. Even when we observe the starry sky—which we certainly can't physically influence—what we see and how we see it is not just an impression of the world. It is, instead, simultaneously influenced by the way in which we express ourselves in the world. It's not for nothing that we say, for example, that "the Ptolemaic world view was an expression of medieval Western culture." And the *Talmud* says: "We see the world not as it is. But as we are".

The human ability—or even necessity—to relate to others therefore becomes apparent not just in impressive, but also in expressive encounters with the world. People do not behave in a way that can be formulated from an external "non-human" point of view. Only a thing or an animal is describable in such a way. People, in contrast, act. The entirety of their expression always takes place in the context of a Lebenswelt that is filled with meaning. This Lebenswelt is populated and structured by other human beings who also act in a meaningful way. It is, therefore, filled by our meaningfulness[4] and by previous generations of structured and modified matter—tools, vehicles, buildings, pictures, books, musical instruments, nuclear power stations, gardens, etc.—and ultimately even with meaningful natural "things", which we enchant with meaning (see chapter 4) through our specific means of observation and through reification alone (see below).

---

context: the more complex the creature's contextual sensitivity, the more complex its structure

[2] the world in which the organism operates.

[3] Gestaltic cycle, a cycle of action and perception in the environment

[4] in other words, the sense of having meaning and purpose

As human beings, it is therefore (according to Watzlawick et al 1967) impossible for us _not_ to act. Even if someone is just "sitting there" without moving, even if he is completely alone, without any other (!) person present in the room, and without any understanding of the possible meanings of this cataleptic stare, this self-reflexive viewpoint of the "_lack of understanding_" itself gives reasons for an understanding—namely of a person who doesn't understand himself. This is because a person is (as Sartre said) condemned to endow himself and his actions in the world with meaning—and, as the case may be, to existentially suffer from a sense-endowed feeling of senselessness. As long as we see such people not just as biological entities but rather as human beings, we assume that they cannot completely exclude themselves from sense and meaning structures. And then, more than ever, others attribute sense and meaning to such a person's actions. Otherwise, the concept of "catalepsy"— which describes something that is noteworthy for people and by this description shapes meaningfully the complex chaos of possibilities of aspects and observations—would not exist.

The impressive and expressive meaningfulness of the human Lebenswelt must by no means remain constantly and extensively in conscious awareness. We can be deep in thought, busy with some fascinating problem or other, and yet still steer a car through traffic. In doing so, we take in road signs, signals, traffic markings, our own position, the movements of other vehicles etc. in a meaningful way; piece them together into a meaningful, complex holistic situation; and act in even more complex, coordinated ways within this situation when we appropriately operate steering wheel, gas pedal, clutch and brake.

Although our conscious awareness may be busy with quite different matters, we accomplish this amazing achievement of being able to act in a coordinated way in largely new complex situations. This shows that our reflexive awareness is not *really* necessary for these kinds of impressions, for the processing of these impressions, and for coordinated behavior (as J. Jaynes, 1988, explained in a more extensive and detailed fashion). Accordingly, parts of our perceptions, of connected thoughts and of feelings and/or actions, can seem strange, incomprehensible or senseless to us—although their meaning is revealed to others. We ourselves, for example by means of therapy, can also open up the true meaning and accordingly learn to better understand "our selves".

These last remarks already lead to the fact that meaningfulness as a necessary basic structure of a human Lebenswelt must in no way be understood only as something positive and favorable. One can even say that everything that leads people to seek psychotherapy is related to the painful aspect of this human ability of wanting and needing to have a Lebenswelt that constitutes a meaningfully structured Gestalt. This expresses itself in two different ways. On the one hand, a felt lack of sense is a great strain. The painful experiences that accompany our life-stories vary from misunderstandings regarding one's own impressive or expressive life processes as just described, to the affliction of living a life that is until now (supposedly) lacking in or completely void of sense (cf. Frankl 1984). Similarly, the struggle between people within a society (and between societies) for sense and for the power to define sense can be seen this way. On the other hand, we are all too often trapped in sense structures that we experience as an oppressive kind of order that restricts and determines the creativity of our life processes.

This is due to the fact that sense and meaning can only be gained by the process of selecting, reducing, and ordering the enormous complexity of the world and of the life processes. Our Lebenswelt is simply not the same world that is thought of by physicists as a world of vast *"streams of stimuli"*. Instead, it's a world that is ordered into figure(s) and ground and Gestalts. Our Lebenswelt is also not composed of myriad fragmented single moments (or indeed of a stream of quanta); rather of comparatively few coherent stories.

If we take the visual perception of a stimulus as an example, then—described from an objective external viewpoint—it is an erratic sequence of discrete fixations of 0.1-0.3 seconds in duration, which are interrupted by eye movements of various kinds (particularly by macro saccades, which are larger but unconscious changes in gaze). Our image of the neighbor we meet every morning for a small chat on the way to the bus stop that lasts, for say 10 minutes, is however in no way "made up" of a sequence of around 4 x 20 = 240 fixated images per minute—or 2400 images per morning, or 876,000 per year. Rather, we have a quite stable schematic image that shows this neighbor "sun tanned" in summer, "rather pale" in winter, sometimes casually and sometimes elegantly clothed—an image that possibly allows us to say something more about the neighbor's appearance over the past year. But this is most certainly not just a sequence of detailed impressions that correspond to those 876,000 single images that were projected onto the retina. Indeed, we are not aware of anything of the saccades that occur between the discrete fixations—instead, when we are looking at our neighbor's face and happen to change our gaze without intention or conscious awareness, we have the impression (!) that our gaze is "at rest".

In the same way, the "objectivity" of myriad single utterances of the neighbor, each comprising many words and phonemes, which are further composed of complex and diverse component frequencies, give rise to something that we experience as part of his biographical life-story. And we arrange this too, into a vague but coherent image of his son, for example, who lives in America.

This detailed example should make it clear how extremely strong this constructive aspect is, with which comparatively simple Gestalts arise from objectively given, enormously complex stimulus configurations. The world of our Lebenswelt is simply not a complex space of incoherent information quanta, rather it is our meaningfully structured, relatively heavily reduced, sufficiently stable, and strongly ordered (by episodes and "stories" or narratives) cognitive domain.

Although this constructive accomplishment is the *foundation* of the every-day world, it is not normally made a subject of discussion *within* the every-day world. Instead, it is taken to be unquestionably "self-evident". This changes only if implicit assumptions which underlie this "self-evidence" are impaired at some point, and people's constructions depart from the normal order of this context, so that we experience their expressions also as a "disorder". In the context of the *professional reconstruction* of the every-day world—which in a way can be seen as the task of psychology, psychopathology and psychotherapy—it is my opinion that we also take this everyday ability far too much for granted. Accordingly, we are amazed by pathological cases and dedicate great attention to them—as was true of Freud over a hundred years ago with his "Psychopathology of Everyday Life" (Freund, 1902, Kriz, 2003). We don't, however, devote much time to the consideration and fascination of how an adequately stable world emerges from the chaos of impressions, and how we manage to agree adequately well with each other in spite of the subjectivity of inner experience(s).

It is therefore just as interesting as the discussion of pathologies to take the highly constructive aspect of our "reality" outlined above into consideration, and to ask the oppositely stated question: "How and to what extent can we actually be sure whether and how much we share the contents of our personal Lebenswelt with others?" Of our daily conflicts and problems with others, we really know how often "differing points of view", controversial "truths", arguments about "how it really was", etc., play a significant role. This is an expression of the contradiction between self-evident reality on the one hand, and the constant scrutiny of this assumed implicitness on the other. How often do we have to laboriously make those apparently implicit aspects of ourselves clear to others and to come to an understanding of them ourselves—and how distressing is it, when these efforts don't succeed, indeed, when we sometimes don't even understand ourselves?

These ordering processes—which can be seen from the perspective of systems theory as an interplay between reductions by attractors or schematizing on the one hand, and completion dynamics on the other hand (see below)—are therefore often distressing because they are not primarily appropriate to that which we really need. Often, they are not suitable to our personal requirements and to the very living of our lives but, on the contrary, they reflect the ordering tendencies of *society*, families and other social organizations to a great extent. Here consequently, slightly conflicting goals can arise—for example when the need for attention can only be met by de-prioritizing oneself. What's more, in some aspects the ordering structures of another person's Lebenswelt are taken over by an individual. Although these ordering structures are important and adequate for this other person, they don't correspond well enough to the life requirements and processes of the individual. Psychoanalysis speaks here of "introjection".

The necessity of these ordering processes for the establishment of our Lebenswelt has already been explained in *"Chaos, Fear, and Order"* (Kriz, 1997). The kernel of this argumentation was to show how our evolutionarily acquired ability of creating and finding regularities in order to avoid the experience of fear makes human life easier on the one hand, and must therefore be appreciated. On the other hand, unnecessary and distressing meaning structures can arise from the over-application and bias of these ordering tendencies, which can partially—or sometimes greatly—restrict the freedom that is won by creating our world.

According to Sartre, we are always "more" than our situation, and this is the ontological foundation of our freedom. We are "condemned" to be free, due to our creatively understanding of our self against the background of a narrative structured time-line of past, present, and future as ordering categories of our experience. On the other hand, these narratives are pre-structured before we step onto life's stage and take our roles. Moreover, the ordering forces of these narratives are embedded in the ordering forces and comprehensive narratives of our social surroundings.

Self-organization and Fields of Meaning

What are the principles, metaphors and ideas that are useful to refer to in order to understand the multi-level dynamic of meaning structures?

As I have argued in the previous chapters, the principles of mechanistic science are a very suitable framework for the task of repairing the *dis-order* of a defective engine. In contrast, those principles turned out to be rather inadequate for an understanding of what is needed in the case of helping living entities and, particularly, for those living entities who are "condemned to endow themselves and their actions in the world with meaning" (Sartre)— namely, the human beings.

Modern theories of self-organization, however, have not only changed our conception of the world but have also turned out to be a valuable source of much more adequate principles that can be used to understand processes in biological, medical, psychological, psychotherapeutic and social fields. For example, the "six characteristics of working with living beings", summarized forty years ago by Wolfgang Metzger (see chapter 4) - earlier discredited by opponents as "lyrical" and "too unscientific" - correspond very well to the principles of modern scientific systems theory as it is described today.

In order to understand the relevance of this perspective for a conception of the actualization of human relationships and a common field of meaning (already mentioned in chapter 5), we first have to make a short detour and take a brief look at Haken's synergetics, which is a particularly fruitful interdisciplinary approach to systems theory and self-organization theory. Again, all mathematical and other technical considerations are omitted as far as possible. However, before we can move on to a discussion of the cognitive and interactive aspects involved in the dynamic of order, we need to at least understand some of the core principles.

Circular causality, order and fields

A central aspect of Synergetics concerns the circular interaction between order parameters on the macroscopic level, and the dynamic on the microscopic level that is enslaved by these order parameters. Typical examples are (without going into much detail here - and omitting examples involving cognitive aspects, which we will discuss in the next paragraph):

- **Laser**: the coherent light wave, which synchronizes the emission of light from the individual atoms in such a way that they contribute to a common light wave;

- **Bénard Instability**: the hexagonal macroscopic, coherent movements in the form of convection "rolls" which "enslave" the movements of the individual molecules in such a way that they contribute to the common pattern of movement;

- **rhythmic applause**: the spontaneously arising common clapping rhythm, which often emerges from the chaos of applause after a concert, synchronizing the individual clapping rhythms in such a way that they contribute to the common rhythm;

- patterns of interaction and interpretations in a "**marriage crises**": the mutual/y structured climate of distrust, insinuation, misrepresentations, and allegations which undermines the benevolent trusting interpretation of actions in such a way that this climate (i.e. cognitive-interactional field) dominates and shapes the thinking, perceiving, interpreting, and acting of each partner, enslaves the patterns of interaction, and contributes in turn to this climate of distrust.

- **Corporate Identity**: the common imagination of the goals, values, and principles of a company (or other organization), which shapes the activities of smaller departments or individuals in such a way that they act in the sense of this imagination and thus contribute to it.

All of these examples have something in common: Order parameters on the macroscopic level—which represent a field of structuring forces—are relatively stable (i.e. if at all, they only change slowly) and "enslave" the microscopic dynamics. *This is the top-down perspective of the interrelation.* At the same time, however, the order parameters (and the field which they represent) are nothing other than abstract structural variables, to which all of the elements on the microscopic level contribute by means of their dynamics. *This is the bottom-up perspective of the interrelation.* Accordingly, the coherent wave of the laser is made up of emitted light(waves) of single atoms; the highly ordered "rolls" of movement in the Bénard Instability are made up of the movements of single molecules; the coherent applause rhythm consists of the hand-clapping of many individuals; the climate of distrust is composed of the interpretations and communications of each partner; and the "corporate identity" consists of the imaginations of the individuals.

During the self-organized formation (so-called "emergence"), these order parameters first develop in relation to competing possibilities of order by means of weak fluctuations. Some of these alternatives of possible order, however, do not represent the overall condition of the system and its surroundings as well as others—as a consequence, they lose the competition and their special contribution to the dynamic becomes weaker and weaker. Other alternatives lose the competition just by chance—the same chance that lets the ball go to the left or to the right side in fig. 6.1a. Both sides are equivalent alternatives. However, chance—in the form of the smallest fluctuations or "the butterfly's wing" (to refer to that famous metaphor)—breaks this symmetry of equivalent alternatives. However, when the ball has left the highly instable point of equilibrium and moves—let's say—a little to the right side by chance, then, by necessity, the ball continues to go to the right side, falling down into the valley, because the forces become stronger and stronger until it reaches the valley. Although in many cases just two alternatives are typical (fig.6.1a), landscapes of many more alternatives are also possible (fig.6.1b).[5]

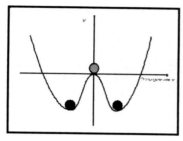

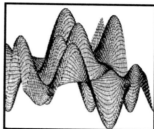

Figure 6.1a   Figure 6.1b

Accordingly, and also in our examples, the forces of order become stronger and stronger while the order establishes, and at the same time more strongly enslave the dynamics of the parts on the micro-level in a circular-causal manner ("autocatalysis"). Although these order parameters emerge in a self-organized fashion, they nevertheless represent the environmental conditions of the system in such a way that they represent one (of two or many) possible adaptations to these external conditions.[6] In most cases, this concerns the minimization or maximization of certain variables (or aspects), which coordinate the relations between the system and its environment. In the case of the laser, this concerns the maximization of the flow of energy; in the case of the Bénard instability, the convection movement becomes a maximum. Similarly, the clapping rhythm supposably[7] concerns the maximization of

---

[5] There can be very many alternatives if one takes multidimensional space with many dimensions or variables into account.
[6] These external conditions are represented by so-called "control parameters".
[7] The examples of rhythmic applause, marriage crisis, and Corporate Identity serve here only to analogously indicate the transferability of

the expressive group feeling; the marriage crisis concerns the maximization of the caution against harm and even more about "being the fool"; and in the case of corporate identity, it is a matter of the maximization of the feeling of coherence and the clarity, in the sense of belonging to the organization in contrast to competitive alternatives.

In the examples mentioned, the central aspect was that the self-organized orders were just in nascence — a so-called emergence.[8] In the fields of psychology and social science, however, there are many phenomena for which it makes sense to assume that the order and their order parameters have developed already before the relevant time-frame of observation, and that these order parameters display their effects now, in the current dynamic.[9] For example, the ordering principles with which an adult structures his relations to the world, to other people, and finally himself can be understood as order parameters, which emerged in early development through self-organization (but, of course, in relation to the environment). Specifically, the structuring principles for human relationships that were discussed within the context of attachment theory (Bowlby 1988) are to be understood in this way.[10]

---

the concepts to such topics. Such a transfer, of course, requires a careful analysis and the definition of the exact processes and operations in order to enable more than mere metaphor. There isn't the space here to do this – I am, however, certain that it is possible, and in the case of the "clapping rhythm" example, this has already been shown to a large extent (see Kriz 1999b, 2004, Néda et al 2000).

[8] The Corporate Identity example should also be understood in this sense.

[9] Elsewhere (Kriz 1997), I have pleaded for the differentiation between (a) structure emergence, e.g. formation of attractors, (b) structure representation through a dynamic process, and (c) structure representation through display.

[10] Some structuring principles – like the figure-ground differentiation, for example – have already even emerged in the process of evolution.

Accordingly, the operators that play a central role in various approaches under the concept of "schema" are normally structuring principles which emerged already years ago. In the current processes of perception, cognitive processing, and expression (including actions and movements), these structuring principles actualize and unfold their shaping forces which act on the new material of cognition.

Already in the work of Bartlett (1932), who coined the term "Schema" and introduced it into psychology, the cognitive reception of complex and new material meant assimilation through existing schemata. Moreover, the act of memory requires an active "process of construction". In this process of remembering, existing schemata *are* used to construct compatible details. (This plays a central role in "Person-Centered System Theory" (Kriz 2004a), in the form of "completion dynamics".)

According to Piaget, who took Bartlett's schema concept and differentiated it further for his developmental psychology, every cognitive activity is an interplay between assimilation and accommodation. Assimilation structures a situation according to already existing schemata. Accommodation, on the other hand, means that the environmental conditions are such that the schemata can no longer adequately work and, therefore, they modify themselves in order to adapt the organism to the new conditions. In the terminology of Synergetics, this is a "phase transition": the system's dynamic abandons an established state of order, passes the gate of chaotic instability and creates a new attractor due to modified environmental conditions (i.e. control parameters). Piaget assumed a hierarchy of schemata, whereby higher-order schemata

However, in our considerations here they play no central role, as we share these principles to a large extent with all people, and they lie outside of our time-frame for self-organization processes.

work as structuring operators on lower schemata—and at the same time, again through circular causality, the higher-order schemata emerge from this process.

The schema concept has the problem, however, that two very different aspects and levels of the process dynamic are often confused with one another: "Schema" is understood by some in the sense of ordering forces, thus meaning the operators or order parameters mentioned above. For others, however, "schema" relates to the developed order, thus to the ordered contents.[11]

For this reason, we prefer the concept of order parameters which defines a field that influences (or even enslaves) the current dynamics. Here, the term "field" is to be understood in purely abstract terms (similarly to the idea of a "variable space" in psychology)—in no way does it require Euclidean space. Accordingly, Gestalt psychology had already referred to Einstein's field definition: "A totality of simultaneously existing facts, which are understood as being reciprocally dependent upon one another, is what one calls a field" (Einstein 1934, after Metzger 1986). The Gestalt psychology of the Berlin School (Wertheimer, Koffka, Köhler) understood "Gestalt" explicitly in the context of such a field conception. This was specifically elaborated by Köhler in the context of his Isomorphy thesis, and by Lewin in the context of (psychological) field theory. These concepts did not only sway Bartlett and Piaget strongly; Haken also explicitly refers to Gestalt psychology in his consideration of psychological phenomena. Accordingly, the connections of these Gestalt aspects with Synergetics are further elaborated in a volume of Tschacher (1997) about "Prozessgestalten" (Gestalt of a Process).

---

[11] Unfortunately, many examples of the misinterpretation of the "schema concept" as ordered *content* can be found in the literature.

Order in the Process of Cognitive Dynamics

Haken (1992), with reference to the circular causality between the field (described by the order parameters) and the micro-level dynamics, emphasized that pattern formation and pattern recognition are to be conceived of as two sides of the same coin. If a part of the subsystems (or elements) is already ordered, a field is generated, which "enslaves" the rest of the system—thus completing the order. From this perspective, pattern *formation* takes place.

Orders are "*recognized*" the other way around, in that some features of the order similarly generate a field (or order parameters), which completes the further characteristics of the order (cf. Fig.6.2 with some of the above examples).

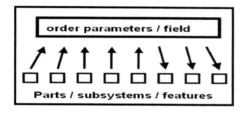

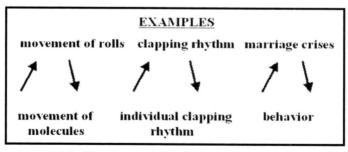

Figure 6.2: Circular causality

The concept of "completion dynamics" is also relevant to cognitive processes. The macroscopic order is reestablished according to the field's order parameters. A classical experiment from Asch (1946) can, for example, be newly interpreted from this perspective. Asch was a proponent of the Gestalt psychological view, and therefore pointed out that the overall impression of a situation or of a stranger is not just a collection of various separate pieces of information. Rather, the given information is seen in a context and thus yields an organized whole.

Therefore, when we look at a person, a certain impression of his character emerges immediately in us. This corresponds to the completion dynamic. In one of Asch's richly varied experiments, a description of a person, in the form of a list of six typical characteristics, was read slowly to students. One group was presented with the following list: "intelligent - industrious - impulsive - critical - stubborn - envious". Another group was given the same list but in reverse order: "envious - stubborn - critical - impulsive - industrious - intelligent". It was shown that the first group had a clearly positive impression of the described person afterwards, while the other group had judged the person in a clearly negative manner.

Often quoted in the literature as a "primacy effect", this finding can also be understood in the light of circular causality or completion dynamics, as shown in Fig.6.2. The first characteristics generate an overall impression, which "enslaves" the interpretation of the further characteristics correspondingly—i.e. each in turn further completing the image of that person. For example, "critically" can be understood in a more positive or in a more negative way—or, more precisely, being part of a positive judged person or part of a negative judged person.

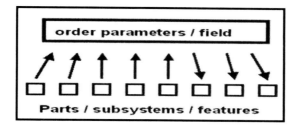

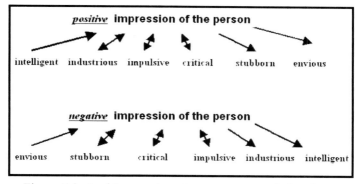

Figure 6.3: Asch's experiment, seen as a completion dynamic in a cognitive field (the directions of the arrows only illustrate the possible main directions of the forces).

These few examples should demonstrate the fruitfulness of the system-theoretical approach and its principles, even when applied to the reconstruction of psychological phenomena, findings, descriptions, and the associated dominant principles. It therefore stands to reason to apply this approach to the investigation of mental and/or affect-logical[12] completion dynamics. To this end, numerous experiments have been conducted in Osnabrück in the

---

[12] I use "affect-logically" here, because the meaning of "cognitive" in former times included the entire cognitive process (thus, naturally, rational *and* affective components), but was then absurdly reduced in psychology to "rational-logical" aspects. As a consequence, one now has to readjust this analytical one-sidedness of this view with creative terms like "cognitive affective".

last 15 years, in which the attracting strength of the affect-logical processes was examined in quite different
contexts (overviews can be found in Kriz 1999a, 2001,
2004b). Although we cannot go into details here, it
should nevertheless be emphasized that in my opinion, an
even larger range of psychological problems could be investigated with such experimental designs. An important
question deals with the question of how "fields" with
structuring operators are created or invoked from single
pieces of information in the cognitive dynamic, which
then lead in the further process to a clear attracted and
completed order, in the sense of an image of "reality".[13]

Order Parameters in the Surroundings of Orders

What then does a meaning field organize? For instance
in Asch's experiment: is the interpretation of the "person"
organized by the field that came up from the attributes
(micro → macro, or bottom-up) or is the meaning of the
attributes organized by the field that came up "down"
from the impression of the whole "person" (macro → micro, or top-down)? Of course, a great number of influences on meaning are always active, operating in the
sense of mutual penetrating and interacting fields. For
example, our understanding of meanings is subject to
social, familial, biographic and general ongoing influences, among other things. This complexity of the aspects
and levels is nothing unusual, however, because self-or-

---

[13] It should however be at least mentioned that many further research
paths exist for the demonstration of the correspondence between system-theoretical and psychological principles. Today, an increasing
number of psychological researchers are involved. Overviews are
given in Haken & Stadler (1990); Tschacher, Schiepek & Brunner
(1992); Schiepek & Tschacher (1997); or Tschacher & Dauwalder
(1999, 2003).

ganization always takes place only relative to the environment of the system. Thus, for example, in the case of patterns of interaction in a family, a variety of influences always take part in the self-organization process— social (including legal aspects); biological and evolutionary; individual biographical; and ongoing. These rules and orders are then predetermined for a family, and (nearly) closed to influence. Of course, these influences naturally play a role when trying to understand a particular interaction pattern in the family. However, it makes sense to focus only on one certain aspect—namely on how such a pattern in the interaction dynamic develops and stabilizes through self-organization (with respect to the influences of the "environment").[14]

In the case of fields of meaning there are also influences on different levels. For example, on the societal level certain categorically reduced themes have already been evolved in our culture, which work as very strong "meaning attractors", as was discussed at length elsewhere (Kriz 1997a, 2004a). These attractors enslave the interpretation and bring about a contraction in the space of perceptions and interpretations in the cognitive processes of individuals, couples and families. As a consequence, people end up with a narrow horizon where alternative options are left out of the view. Typical themes, operating as such malignant "meaning attractors" often narrow the options of interpretation and action, are for example "good"–"bad", "true"–"false", "sick"–"healthy", "guilty"–"innocent", "correct"–"incorrect", "right"– "wrong", etc. Theses themes, of course, refer to great and important aspects of orientation in the life of human beings. However, they develop malignant power when they

---

[14] And, *in the case of a family*, this can be the interpretation and actual conversion and commitment of these given social or biological rules – a distinction *important* for therapy!

are understood in a totalitarian way (Kriz, 2004a). In addition, there are many other fields of meaning in language, culture, and society which cannot be modified a great deal by individuals within a short time.

For the following, it is interesting to analyze how fields of meaning in communication develop through self-organization relative to such fields of meaning and sense attractors that are already in existence. We will take the communication between only two people as a central example (e.g. a couple or a patient and therapist). It is easy to see, however, that these principles can be extended to communications involving more than two people.

Our starting point is the fact that communication always contains two sub-processes: the process of "*incitation*" and the process of "*excitation*", as Nørretranders (1997) puts it. The words which one person says to another represent a very large amount of "meaning information", which exists consciously and unconsciously "in the head" of the speaker, and is "infolded" more or less into the spoken words. In doing so, certain aspects are selected and others discarded and information is condensed. However, at the same time some aspects are simultaneously unfolded and developed and "appropriate" words and metaphors are sought. This information, condensed by "incitation", is now voiced and, in the process of understanding, excited by the listener, i.e. unfolded. This "tree of speech" is roughly illustrated in Fig. 6.4.[15]

---

[15] Here, the structuring rules of the metaphors of speaking and understanding (which are overlooked far too often) should be taken into account. These are very concisely elaborated in Jaynes (1993), with reference to the "characteristics of consciousness": Spatialization, Excerption, the Analog 'I', the Metaphor 'Me', Narratization and Conciliation (for details, see Jaynes 1993).

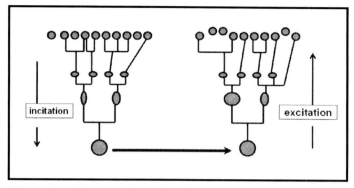

Figure 6.4: The tree of speech (after Nørretranders 1997)

Along with all of this ,it must however be considered that "verbalizing " and "listening" as a rule regard a small portion of a longer process, in which both partners are involved by means of diverse feedback loops. As a consequence, that which the "verbalizer" has "in his head" (in the broadest sense) at a particular instant—i.e. the meaning which he would like to communicate and has to incitate—depends on many aspects. Besides the above mentioned common fields of meaning in society (i.e. the rather "general" meanings of the words, for example), it also depends on the preceding course of the communication. This determines what actually comes to his mind, what he assumes to be meaningful to the listener, what he chooses, etc.

Even stronger, though, is the influence of previous experience in the case of the excitation of the listener. Naturally, he doesn't necessarily unfold his meaning according to the meaning in the head of the speaker (inside of which the listener obviously can't see; otherwise one wouldn't need to communicate). Rather, he excitates according to the cognitive ordering processes in his own head—and these often have a lot to do with his own biography—rather than giving consideration to the message or to the meaning in the speaker's head.

As was elaborated elsewhere (Kriz 1997a)—and as it has been similarly described by numerous other authors — even the words of the speaker can often act as a sort of trigger for starting "inner movies". Here then, the excitation is almost stimulus invariant: what is activated (and which will then be responded to), is that which one wants to hear, i.e. the meaning that is *assumed*. And people all too often no longer check back whether this meaning is also seen in the same way by the other person. This process—which almost completely makes up the "daily bread" of couple and family therapists—can be illustrated by the sequence where the therapist asks the woman in a relationship counseling session: "Did you hear what your partner just said?" and she answers "No, I didn't—but by the way he looked at me, I already knew what he would say!".

On the other hand however, a communication that succeeds sufficiently well means that a *common* field of meaning emerges from the many running feedback loops (including the expectation of the expectation regarding the interpretation of meaning). This field governs both that on which both actually focus the conversation, and the processes of incitation and excitation. During the course of the communication, a more or less exclusive shared field of meaning thus emerges between both partners. This exclusivity perhaps becomes clearest, when it is obvious to both that the whimsical expression of an "Olé!" is an allusion to a bullfight during last summer's holiday in Spain, which may have been followed by a particularly lovely evening spent together. In this example, there are certainly further aspects that both partners unfold in a similar manner. However, there are other aspects that each partner unfolds in their own more private and individual way—connected with non-shared associations.

To the outsider who didn't take part in the development of this common field of meaning, the meaning of the "Olé!" remains largely cryptic. If necessary, he can indeed excitate something from *his* experience of life that makes sense to *him*. And when he now communicates this, a common field of meaning develops, to which *all three* persons contribute. At the same time, however, this example makes it clear that in a field of meaning, different substructures can be active for the individual participants. For example, the third person could probably never participate in *all* of the *commonly* excitated meanings of the *couple*. And in the same way, the couple cannot participate in *all* excitated meanings of each individual partner. Communication is just—in the actual sense of the word *communio*—a larger or smaller participation in a field of meaning that is developed in common. In no way, however, is it the possession of all meanings of the other (and certainly not a possession of "the truth"!).

It should now be clear, that the emergence of a common field of meaning of two (or more) partners and the ordering processes of incitation and excitation, can by all means be described in terms of Synergetics, with its circular causality, order parameters, and completion dynamic. Figures 6.2 and 6.3 can now be modified into Figure 6.5:

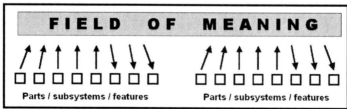

Figure 6.5: Two (or more) people develop a common field of meaning

The question, which can again be discussed here only briefly, of when the self-organization processes which generate a common field of meaning are particularly effective, can be answered similarly to the question of the efficacy of order parameters in general. They are more effective the less the dynamic is influenced by other fields. So, for example, the strange forces of fields whose effect we describe as "neurosis" can hardly become effective when the situation is strongly pre-structured. For instance, when one submits a tax declaration to the tax office: The office and the space itself, officials, filled out forms, and the subject-matter (the tax declaration) are so clearly structured that the interaction dynamic will be dominated (one can by all means say "enslaved") by this. Quite contrary to this, in a very unstructured situation— for instance on the psychoanalyst's couch or while getting to know a new partner—it is exactly those neurotic field forces that are effective (and so are open to experience and observation).

Accordingly, the probability is low that a common field of meaning will self-organize when the meanings are already strongly pre-structured—for instance when the conversation is characterized by clear logical deductions, definitions, use of simple facts, etc. (shared by both parties). Then on the one hand, hardly any reduction in complexity is needed, and/or the rules of the incitation and excitation are explicitly and normatively set.[16]

Then again, reputed therapists such as Rogers, Erickson or Gilligan pointed out how the emergence of a common field of meaning is necessary in the case of higher polyvalence, uncertainty, and lack of clarity. Such a situation, on the other hand, is often experienced as a very

---

[16] In terms of Julius Kuhl's (2001) Psi Theory: when left hemispherical object recognition predominates and right hemispherical complex networked processes is less important.

"close" relationship which can develop an almost astonishing power. This is (likewise in agreement with many therapists) only then possible when the complex situation of common development and adjustment of meanings is characterized by openness and mutual high regard—i.e. when neither of the partners has the power to define terms, and no strong hierarchical difference exists[17].

In closing, it should still be pointed out that the development (and modification) of common fields of meaning can be facilitated by means of techniques, which allow communication of aspects of the fields of meaning not only verbally by linguistic incitation and excitation, but rather through visualizing and experiencing. For this, artistic techniques—painting, music, poetry etc.—are equally as helpful, as is visualization in space[18], that is, the various techniques of sculpture-work and psychodrama. In all of these techniques, meanings can be pointed out in a deictic way, so to speak, and the common imagination need not only be employed "in the head", rather it can be looked at. This is not to say that the still important components of the process of incitation and excitation may be underestimated: because naturally, a picture or a sculpture doesn't simply speak "for itself", but only to the people who seek and construct meaning.

---

[17] Meynhardt (2004), by the way, pointed out these aspects in a similar way through the differentiation of knowledge which concerns facts and objective data on the one hand, and knowledge which concerns values on the other hand. From our perspective, the latter serves as an order parameter in a polyvalent, highly complex, less objective pre-structured situation.

[18] This corresponds to the "spatialization" in Jaynes – see footnote 15

References

Asch, S. (1946): Forming impressions of personality. Journal of Abnormal and Social Psychology, 41, 258-290

Bartlett, F.C. (1932). Remembering. Cambridge: Cambridge Univ. Press.

Bowlby, J. (1988). A secure Base. Clinical applications of attachment theory. London: Routledge

Brunner, E. J. (2002) Organisationsberatung lernen. Freiburg: Lambertus

Forrester, Jay W. (1961): Urban Dynamics. Cambridge: MIT-Press

Forrester, J.W. 1972: Grundzüge einer Systemtheorie (Principles of Systems). Wiesbaden: Gabler

Frankl, V. (1984) Man's search for Meaning. New York: Simon & Schuster

Freud, S. (1902/54) Zur Psychopathologie des Alltagslebens. Fischer, Frankfurt 1954

Goffman, Erving (1963): Asylums. Essay on the Social Situation of Mental Patients and Other Inmates. Chicago: Aldine

Greif, Siegfried (1994): Handlungstheorie und Selbstorganisationstheorien. In: P.Richter & B. Bergmann (Hrsg): Die Handlungsregulationstheorie. Göttingen: Verlag f. Angewandte Psychologie. 89 - 114

Greif, Siegfried (1996): Teamfähigkeiten und Selbstorganisationskompetenzen. In: S.Greif & H.-J- Kurtz (Hrsg): Handbuch selbstorganisiertes Lernen. Göttingen: Verlag f. Angewandte Psychologie. 161 - 178

Haken, H. (1981): Synergetics. An introducion. Berlin: Springer.

Haken, H. (1984): Erfolgsgeheimnisse der Natur. Synergetik: Die Lehre vom Zusammenwirken. Frankfurt/M: Ullstein.

Haken, H. (1992): Synergetics in Psychology. in: Tschacher, W., Schiepek, G. & Brunner, E. J. (eds): Selforganization and Clinical Psychology. Berlin: Springer, 32-54

Haken, H. & Stadler, M. (1990): Synergetics of cognition. Berlin: Springer

Heisenberg, W. (1955): Das Naturbild der heutigen Physik. Hamburg: Rowohlt

Jaynes, J. (1993): Der Ursprung des Bewusstseins. Reinbek: rororo

Kriz, J. (1996): Chaos und Selbstorganisation. In: Greif, S. & Kurtz H-J. (Hrsg.): Handbuch Selbstorganisiertes Lernen. Göttingen: Verlag für angewandte Psychologie, 33-43

Kriz, J. (1997): Attraktoren bei kognitiven und sozialen Prozessen. Kritische Analyse eines Mode-Konzepts. In: G. Schiepek & W. Tschacher (Hrsg.) Selbstorganisation in Psychologie und Psychiatrie. Braunschweig: Vieweg, 57-70

Kriz, J. (1997a): Chaos, Angst und Ordnung. Wie wir unsere Lebenswelt gestalten. Göttingen: Vandenheock

Kriz, J. (1997b): Selbstorganisation als Grundlage lernender Organisationen. In: Wieselhuber & Partner (Hrsg.) Handbuch lernende Organisation. Wiesbaden: Gabler, 187-196.

Kriz, J. (1999a): Systemtheorie für Psychotherapeuten, Psychologen und Mediziner. UTB/Facultas)

Kriz, J. (1999b): On Attractors - The Teleological Principle in Systems Theory, the Arts and Therapy. POIESIS. A Journal of the Arts and Communication, 24-29

Kriz, J. (2001):Self-Organization of Cognitive and Interactional Processes. In: Matthies, M., Malchow, H. & Kriz, J. (Eds): Integrative Systems Approaches to Natural and Social Dynamics. Heidelberg: Springer, 517-537

Kriz, J. (2003): Kriz, Jürgen (2003): Versagen: Desaster oder Aufbruch? In: B. Boothe & W. Marx (eds.) Panne – Irrtum - Missgeschick. Die Psychopathologie des Alltagslebens in interdisziplinärer Perspektive. Bern: H. Huber, 163 - 176

Kriz, J. (2004a): Personzentrierte Systemtheorie. Grundfragen und Kernaspekte. In: Schlippe, A.v. & Kriz, W.C. (Hrsg): Personzentrierung und Systemtheorie. Göttingen: Vandenhoeck & Ruprecht, 13 – 67

Kriz, J. (2004b): Beobachtung von Ordnungsbildungen in der Psychologie: Sinnattraktoren in der Serielle Reproduktion. In: Moser, S. (Hg): Konstruktivistisch Forschen. Wiesbaden: VS Verlag für Sozialwissenschaften, 43 – 66

Kuhl, J. (2001): Motivation und Persönlichkeit. Interaktionen psychischer Systeme. Göttingen: Hogrefe

Metzger, W. (1986). Gestaltpsychologie. Ausgewählte Werke aus den Jahren 1950-1982. In: M. Stadler & H. Crabus (Hrsg.) Frankfurt/M.: Kramer

Meynhardt, T. (2004) Wertwissen: Was Organisationen wirklich bewegt. Münster/New York: Waxmann

Néda, Z., et al. (2000) Self-organizing processes: The sound of many hands clapping. Nature 403, 849 - 850

Nørretranders, T. (1997): Spüre die Welt. Die Wissenschaft vom Bewußtsein. Reinbek, Rowohlt

Piaget, J. (1976). Die Äquilibration der kognitiven Strukturen. Stuttgart: Pieper.

v.Schlippe, A. & Kriz, J. (1996): Das "Auftragskarussell" Eine Möglichkeit der Selbstsupervision in systemischer Therapie und Beratung. System Familie, 9, 3, 106-110

Schiepek, G. & Tschacher, W. (1997): Selbstorganisation in Psychologie und Psychiatrie. Braunschweig: Vieweg

Tschacher, W. (1997): Prozessgestalten. Göttingen: Hogrefe.

Tschacher, W. & Dauwalder, J.P. (1999): New Jersey: World Scientific

Tschacher, W. & Dauwalder, J.P. (2003): The Dynamical Systems Approach to Cognition. New Jersey: World Scientific

Tschacher, W., Schiepek, G. & Brunner, E. J. (1992): Self-organization and Clinical Psychology Berlin: Springer

Watzlawick P, Beavin JH, Jackson DD (1967) Pragmatics of Human Communication. New York: Norton & Company

Chapter **7**

THE EFFECTIVENESS
OF THE
HUMANISTIC PSYCHOLOGICAL
APPROACH

In the last decades, some Nobel prizes have been awarded for concepts dealing with self-organization in the natural sciences. Correspondingly, the interdisciplinary discourse on systems theory has had a growing influence on many disciplines. If we consider psychology to be the science dealing with the most complex system on earth—namely the self-reflexive, creative-imaginative human being, influenced by processes on different levels such as society and its culture, as well as the physiology and biology of the body and, moreover, by the most complex biological system, namely the human brain—then it is quite remarkable to notice that psychology to a great extent uses rather reductive, simple, mechanistic models of cause and effect of the 19th century and refers to principles and metaphors which became obscure in the natural sciences in the 20th century.

Proof was given that some fundamental principles of the mechanistic age are—at least in such general terms as were tacitly assumed—simply false. These principles work only under very restricted conditions and constraints, which are adequate for machines but, as it turned out, inadequate for entities where complex recursive processes are essential. This is true for living beings and, to an even greater extent, for human beings (because of their self-reflexive consciousness, which changes behavior into action based on thoughts and images of future action).

But it is not only the adequacy of concepts and principles in psychology that must be critically scrutinized in order to understand processes beyond the laboratory and its artificial restrictive conditions (although, without any doubt, these procedures are of value for the investigation of many questions for which these constraints are adequate). Moreover, it is a problem that the more complex and less reductive approaches like the concepts of humanistic psychology are devalued for not being "scientific" or "effective".

As a consequence, I felt the need to publish some papers to encourage people not to reduce their world of living (or their world of understanding) to the adequacy of a lab in order to be "scientific" and to prevent devaluation of their thoughts and work. In contrast, I want to encourage people to enter the discourses on "science", "effectiveness", "quality" etc. courageously.

In the program for this, the 3rd meeting of the German Psychological Association (BDP), the organizing committee have briefly but succinctly—and in my opinion very accurately—described the current Zeitgeist:

"Our society of growth is shaped by the quest for effectiveness and efficiency. Goals should be realized in the shortest possible time and with a minimal expense of

*energy and effort. Behind all this lies the intention to mi-
nimize costs and maximize profits. Social abilities and
skills, and sensibility towards self and others are fre-
quently left behind..."*

As a matter of fact, the "economistic"[1] priority of profit maximization also brings psychologists, psychotherapists, and psychology into a problematic situation. With a
focus on efficacy alone—and, as I'll show, with a very
one-sided meaning of effectiveness at that—many psychologists and psychotherapists find it extremely difficult
to fit the so-called "inherent necessities" of our social and
health system. These "necessities" result in the devaluation of certain aspects of living, which were, once upon a
time, almost essential for the career choice of psychologist or therapist, and have now become untenable luxu-
ries. Here I'm speaking of qualities such as humanity,
sensitivity, empathy, positive regard, and a personal relationship in professional encounters, among others. What's
more, the practitioner who has these qualities should be
ashamed of himself for being "ineffective" (and this is
often still equated with being under-qualified)—or at the
very least should seek to "further qualify" himself.

This compulsion towards efficacy was passed on to
psychology as science in the form of a demand that psychology should primarily devote itself to such questions.
This can be observed, for example, in the current debate

---

[1] By "economistic" – in contrast to "economic or economical" – I
mean the current trend for typically short-term and partitioned profit
maximization. Economistic behavior neglects an extensive honest
balancing of accounts that also considers long-term effects. It ignores
the fact that many psychosocial benefits which are currently suffering
from cutbacks would also arguably be "taken into account" if there
were a fair economic calculation. However, such benefits appear to be
"ineffective" and "uneconom(ist)ic" when costs – e.g. for illness, su-
perannuation, etc. – can be passed on to the general public and de-
layed until "later", while in the short term, profits are skimmed off
privately.

concerning the efficacy of psychotherapy, as considered only from the perspective of evidence based medicine (ebm). Some of the questions that arose as a result—for example, regarding which form of psychotherapy and how much of it the social security system should pay for —are unquestionably important and require careful discussion (far more careful, incidentally, than is actually taking place in the slipstream left by the egoistic interests of the small power-groups involved). But by debating almost exclusively these questions, it seems that certain programs that are intended to support personal development for example, or individuation, or other such (economistically) "unproductive" ideas, have actually become discredited in the process (even though nobody actually expected that the social security system should pay). All that has been painstakingly achieved by psychology in the last hundred years - the lengthy catalog of the capabilities and achievements of the advancement of human development - is in danger of being reduced almost exclusively to an "elimination of symptoms". Accordingly, we are confronted with the argument: "what cannot be calculated and proven to bring or save more money in a shorter time is also worth nothing, and should therefore under no circumstances be seriously pursued any further."

In the rush and bustle of such short-sighted arguments which honor the Zeitgeist, even simple structural contexts are also often overlooked. In this way, for example, a number of perfectly serious therapeutic approaches were accused of having provided insufficient scientific evidence—or no evidence at all—for their efficacy. It may be acceptable to hear this from health politicians, but when scientists raise such accusations, one has to ask if something is being ignored here—namely that the task of producing evidence for or against effectiveness is not one for therapists, rather for scientists. Consequently, it's not an omission on the part of the "therapeutic schools" (whoever may be meant by that); instead, it is the fault of the scientists. They are responsible for the lack of research—particularly concerning those approaches that have spread considerably among the practitioners in the last decades. In spite of this, the representatives of these criticized therapeutic approaches often react in a subdued, embarrassed, and apparently guilty way, instead of loudly denouncing the shortfall of the "critical" scientists. They also neglect to ask where the billions of Euro of tax-payers' money have actually gone, given that no evidence for the effectiveness or ineffectiveness of the psychotherapeutic approach—let's call "X"—has yet been put forward. The (understandable) career and publication dependent preference for a certain kind of hypothesis and experimental design that is found in mainstream psychological research is as a consequence now being suddenly elevated to the position of politically defining health standards, and any omissions are being blamed on those who are not yet actually responsible for research—neither financially or institutionally. And this sleight of hand is obviously working very well!

It is also a sign of the times when the confusion surrounding "effectiveness" gives priority to certain approaches that involve operationalization and measurability—for example, when technological medicine, focused on pieces of apparatus and machines and its directly measurable effects, is judged to be much more effective than apparently "vague" preventative interventions because their effects are much more difficult to measure. But is it really a matter of effectiveness, when for example the victim of a failed suicide attempt who has already been lying in a coma for months without hope of recovery and at a cost of millions, is denied a natural death because of the machines keeping him alive, while at the same time the resources and staff in many institutions devoted to reducing the number of such suicides are subject to sizeable cuts. Or isn't it even more important to consider that the groups promoting technology intensive medicine have more money than those promoting preventative social therapy, and thus have better lobby groups in the governments?

These questions show that by taking the usual interpretation of "effectiveness", the situation—which seems so clear and unambiguous during public debate—is not so straightforward. I don't however want to pursue these questions any further. Rather, I would like to move on to a much more central problem in the ideology of effectiveness. When we permit the "figure of thought" which constructs a contrast between effectiveness and humanity, then by accepting this play on words and thought we are already in a weakened position. If we are pleading for the humane—and, for example, for humanistic psychology—then from the perspective of this contrast, we must defend ourselves and apologize for not being (more) effective. We may perhaps justify this obvious lack of professionalism or scientific foundation by appeal to personal preference, ethical motives, or whatever else, but at the same time we have also acquired the appearance of not satisfying apparently reasonable demands. We then become shamed into submission or silence, and troubled by self-doubt, because we "feel" and "believe" something that evidently is not accepted and rationally grounded, or at least is not effective.

But the title of my paper is *not* "How can we remain effective in spite of a humanistic approach" (or vice versa). Rather, I have deliberately broken through the pseudo-alternative, and spoken about the "effectiveness of the humanistic approach". As is shown by the modern natural sciences—particularly if we consider systems theory which is based on the natural sciences—it is precisely those principles that are essential for "the humanistic approach" that are effective. Indeed, in the technological transfer of system theoretical discoveries to industrial use, which has become increasingly important in physical and chemical technology for example, these "humanistic" principles must be taken into consideration in order for these technologies to really become effective.

What do I mean in this context by "humanistic" principles? Perhaps the easiest way to explain this is by reference[2] to (a reduced version of) "the six characteristics of working with living beings", which were formulated by the Gestalt psychologist Wolfgang Metzger in 1962 (see chapter 4). It is also worth mentioning here that I am convinced that every practitioner in the field of psychotherapy should (and if he is not unsuccessful: does[3]) take these characteristics into account.

One could try to disparage these "characteristics" by branding them as an expression of "over-enthusiasm" on the part of humanistic psychology, and claiming that they are missing any "scientific basis". Some presumptuous "go-getters" have indeed tried to "argue" this way. However, a few years after Metzger's synopsis of these characteristics from the perspective of Gestalt and Humanistic psychology, modern chaos and system theory began its rapid development in the natural sciences. The importance of this development has perhaps been most obviously evidenced by Nobel Prize wins (in other words, a wider recognition by the mainstream of the scientific community within the natural sciences). Amazingly, this new development stresses that exactly those principles (in contrast to some principles of the classical approach in science) corresponding to Metzger's "characteristics" are

---

[2] discussed in more detail in Walter 1985, cf. Kriz 1994
[3] Although the "official" understanding of the process may, according to the particular school, follow other concepts and discuss other theoretical and technical terms.

the essential principles.

But before I get to systems theory in the narrower sense, I would first like to pick up on another long-standing ideological misunderstanding that is important in this context—namely the misinterpretation of "growth". In the text of the organizing committee (mentioned at the beginning), the following question is posed: "Can psychology resist the unfettered focus on growth in some way, and if so—how?" I would like to reply that we can orient ourselves towards "growth" in nature—that is, we can focus on exactly the field from which the idea of growth was first borrowed, and then improperly reinterpreted.

If we look at trees[4], for example, then we see that the essence of growth is in no way a matter of the accumulation of "more and more" of something—for instance of wood or biomass. Such increases do admittedly play a role, particularly in the early stages, but are of minor importance when compared with the aspect of the development of possibilities, or with the constantly renewed adaptation to environmental conditions, or with the "die and become" as Goethe put it (seen, for example, in deciduous trees with their loss of leaves in Fall and budding of new leaves in Spring). It is exactly these aspects that are meant by the concept of "personality growth" for instance (and not a hypertrophied "more and more"). Our economic representatives (and their political lackeys) have certainly perverted this essential qualitative aspect of growth and turned it into something purely quantitative. From their perspective, growth is only a matter of increasing existing quantities, measured in percentages (and "die" would then be nothing more than an unpleasant decrease in this number). Given a planet, which is something that cannot physically increase in size and in

---

[4] further elaborated in Kriz 1993

any case seems to be at maximum load with respect to some aspects (ozone depletion, pollution, exploitation of natural resources), it is in fact necessary to fiercely oppose this growth ideology. With a conception of growth that is in accordance and in tune with nature, however, we have nothing to worry about!

We now come—very briefly[5]—to the essentials of systems theory (based in science)[6], because these (not coincidentally) have a lot to do with the aforementioned "natural" growth. Here we are concerned with phenomena such as "chemical clocks". These chemical reactions, by now quite famous, don't uniquely connect specific reagents with definite results; rather these reactions proceed dynamically, developing spreading patterns over space and time, and changing the chemical context in a particular place in periodic oscillations. With corresponding admixtures, other features like the color can also periodically change, let's say: red-blue-red-blue-red... like the pendulum of a clock—hence the name "chemical clock". Another phenomenon that is possibly even more generally known is the LASER—a system that emits extreme coherent light(waves), that can be so sharply focused that objects can be cut with it (an application which has by now been used in the fields of medicine or technology for many different functions and in many variations).

I would like, however, to explain the essential principles using an even simpler system, the so-called Bénard Instability. As a psychologist, my choice to use a physical system and not the dynamics of a family as an example is due to the fact that such a physical system is more easily definable and less complicated, and can also be looked at

---

[5] for more detail see e.g. Kriz 1992, Kriz 1997a
[6] it should be noted that there are other narratives and discourses which use or refer to the term "systems theory", discussed especially in some philosophical and sociological groups.

with much more ideological detachment than a family.

The phenomenon of Bénard cells was already known and described almost one hundred years ago, but was first theoretically explained during the development of modern systems theory. The underlying facts are easy to describe: a liquid in a circular container is heated from below, and as is the case when you heat water on the stove at home, the difference in temperature between the warmer fluid at the bottom and the cooler surface is equalized by convection currents. This means that hot—and thus lighter—parts move upwards, and colder—thus heavier—parts move downwards. By continually increasing the heat[7], a critical value can be found, at which point a sudden, qualitative change takes place—an ordered movement of the entire liquid in the form of macroscopic rolling movements, which are called "convection rolls". Uncountably many molecules are cooperatively involved in each rolling movement (as shown schematically in Fig. 7.1a). What is even more interesting is that the rolling movements typically take on the complicated shape of a honeycomb pattern (seen from above in Fig. 7.1b).

The Bénard Instability can be seen as a simple but typical example of self-organization, because the liquid forms this macroscopic structure (which, as we will later discuss, can be described as the order parameter of a field) from itself. This order is not introduced as "order" by external factors, for instance by someone stirring the liquid in such a way as to make the rolling movements appear (as was typically thought in the "classical" understanding of intervention).

---

[7] or more precisely, the difference in temperature found at the bottom of the container and at the surface. Therefore, if you just use water, you would have to cool the surface in order to compensate for the large convection movement. However, using special oils (which allow for less convection), it suffices to heat the container from below.

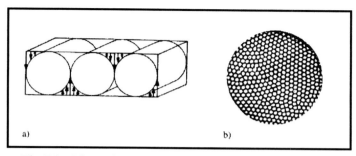

Fig.7.1: The Bénard Instability. (a) Rolling movements (schematic view from the side), (b) honeycomb shaped rolling patterns (seen from above).

Instead, quite unspecific conditions of the system's surroundings (here: the difference in temperature) lead to the self-organization of this highly differentiated dynamical structure, which must be understood as an inherent ordering structure of the system itself. A designer, for example, may want to see eight-sided rolling movements (instead of six-sided), because he thinks that this would be much more "aesthetic" or "creative"—but as eight-sided rolling movements are not in the inherent structure of the system, they cannot be produced.

Similarly, the "designers of animal behavior" (i.e. tamers) had to learn that they could shape the behavior of a raccoon very well by "operant conditioning"—as long as the raccoon was, for example, dealing with one single coin (so the space of possibilities is rather big). However, giving the raccoon two coins means that "nature" works in another way: the raccoon will rub the two coins together—that is its inherent possibility when dealing with two coins. Therefore, it is not a question of ethics but of effectiveness to refrain from attempting to impose any "behavior-order" on a raccoon.

As a consequence, even with regard to animal behavior, scientists had to learn that they must respect inherent structural forces and that they cannot teach, shape or design everything without any limitations. Accordingly, Humanistic Psychologists stress the point that this is not only true for raccoons but also for human beings: many inherent structures—on the evolutionary and biological level as well as on the biographic and cultural level— have to be respected. And again, it is not only a question of ethics but also one of effectiveness.

What makes the crucial difference between the effectiveness in dealing with systems from the modern perspective of systems science, and the idea of effectiveness in everyday life, which is still strongly governed by the ideologies of classical mechanistic Western science (and which, in accordance, governs the cognitive world of far too many psychologists and doctors)?

The classical mechanistic Western ideology was determined through interactions with dead material in artificially isolated systems. From this perspective, all parts of the world and the mechanisms (!) of change can be described by the laws of mechanics. This almost perfectly fits the equally artificial realm of technical instruments and machines. Even "movement" and "change" are understood as being static[8] because non-linear jumps in the development, emergence of new features etc., which ere essential for complex systems—especially living systems—are beyond the conception of the classical model. Dealing with such "classical" systems is therefore a matter of "tin can ideology", as I once put it.[9] From the perspective of that ideology, one can take a dented tin can whose shape is not acceptable due to its "dis-order", and remove the dents (i.e. establish "order") or impose any number of other design ideas upon it. You could, for ex-

---

[8]In fact, thermodynamics could even be renamed thermostatics from the viewpoint of today's dynamical systems research.
[9]cf. Kriz 1986

ample, press it into an Easter bunny shape. Local, causal effects are then typical and successful, and there is a high correlation between the magnitude and direction of energy expended and the result.

For removing dents of a tin can this procedure is undoubtedly effective. However, it can be asked if this procedure is the best metaphor for all kind of intervention.

In the 20th century, and even more so in the last decades, natural science has had to realize that the typical classical systems—which are isolated and non-recursive—can, at best, only give an appropriate model of nature for restricted cases in particular areas and over a short time span. As soon as one broadens the scope of such systems—especially when one takes the dynamics of feedback into account—the characteristic essentials of systems theory apply. This is already necessary for the ever-growing subject areas that deal with interacting systems of dead material. For the life sciences—i.e. biology, medicine, psychology etc.—ignoring feedback in the systems being studied can lead to fundamental confusions. The systems that are observed in the life sciences were not "made" by humans under restricted artificial technical conditions, but they evolved in our natural world. And this is also true for systems which evolve in a comparatively short period of time, as in the case of ontogenesis or sociogenesis, the genesis of a couple structure, pathogenesis, etc.

Furthermore, living systems do not "function" under isolated environmental conditions that can be kept constant by artificial means. On the contrary, these systems are self-organized, and their essential functional capability lies in their ability to adapt to changes in environmental conditions (or better: to realize a dynamic co-evolution in the face of these reciprocal changes).

Systems theory, then, investigates and discusses self-organized systems whose dynamical structures are supported and facilitated by interventions, but ultimately cannot be "made" (unlike the tin Easter bunny). And dealing with such systems is a fundamentally different matter. Even a waterfall, unlike a tin can, cannot be "smoothed out" with a hammer or some other tool when its shape or structure is not to someone's liking. More successful—in other words: effective—interventions must therefore take the intrinsic structure (or even better: the space of possible intrinsic structures) of the system into account. The "history" and the developmental stage of the system must, as we've seen, be taken into consideration—and depending on the stage the system is in, the "same" intervention can have a greater or lesser effect. In sensitive phases of the development of the system, small interventions may suffice to bring about a large and fast qualitative change; while even strong "inputs" may show no effect in stable phases.

In short, exactly those principles which were characterized above as principles of Humanistic Psychology—and summarized by Metzger as characteristics of working with living beings—must be taken into account when dealing with physical or chemical "dead" systems (unless these systems are isolated and feedback free) if the scientists concerned with these systems want to be "effective". This correspondence should become ever clearer when we put together the essential aspects once again (see Table 1 in chapter 4).

Strictly speaking, all of this is actually nothing new and exciting. People have been aware of this—at least implicitly—for centuries in the essential experiential areas of life. And people went along with these principles when they benefited from "nature" and didn't want to cause any damage. Every farmer and gardener, for example, knows that the order they see develop is not "made" like tin Easter bunnies, and that their task is not to encourage accelerated growth of their plants by impatiently pruning them, or to trim the leaves of a "diseased" tree into the "correct" shape with a pair of nail scissors. All of these attempts would be just as absurd as they are ineffective.

This doesn't mean, however, that man is condemned to idleness. Rather, "effectiveness" calls for an exact mixture of permissiveness, tolerance, respect for intrinsic forms and dynamics, sensitivity in choosing the right moment in order to facilitate the systems dynamic by providing for favorable conditions in the system's environment.

It is exactly this that mothers have done with their growing fetuses for thousands of years. It's possible to surgically remove the fetus after 5 months, and to use all the techniques of modern medical technology—perhaps further optimized with artificial insemination—to get more children in a shorter time from the same mother. But this area has so far been spared from this kind of recently propagated idea of "effectiveness", thank goodness.[10]

The new scientific findings are therefore much less surprising than the fact that—contrary to the experience of the majority of people on this planet—the only "source" of order that has been researched and propagated by Western science concerns its production and control, and that scientific efforts have been devoted extensively to the breakdown of order (within the scope of thermodynamics). This is certainly not insignificantly connected to the fact that a manufactured and monitored order suits the interests of those in power much better than a concept of autonomous, self-organized order.

Correspondingly, one of the central dominating themes

---

[10] Although, maybe it's not completely spared, when one considers the sperm bank with sperm from Nobel prizewinner, which has already been used by "simple-minded" women.

of classical Western science and technology was—and still is—Vico's verdict of 1710: *verum et factum convertuntur* (the true and the made are convertible). Hans Primas from ETH-Zurich is equally critical: "In today's scientific practice, producibility and feasibility are in the end the de facto criterium for correctness in scientific thinking" (Primas 1995, p.212). And in the book "Chaos, Fear and Order" (Kriz 1997b), I showed how the necessary human ability to avoid fear-inducing chaos and establish order is, in general, very easily taken too far, and can lead to compulsive ordering. I also pointed out that exactly this fantasy of control was seen during the very early days of Western science, in the work of the "founding fathers" Bacon, Descartes and Newton. This was again a defense against fear—fear of the archaic female way of understanding and approaching the world (for example in the form of the alternative knowledge of witches), of uniqueness and of the uncontrollable.

Although I don't want to explain this again here, it is still notable how surprisingly well the mechanisms that we interpret as typical symptoms in a compulsive patient's defense against fear and anxiety correspond to the principles lauded as "virtues" of a clean and faultless methodology by Western science—and also by psychology textbooks. These principles[11] are:

---

[11]Abraham Maslow, one of the fathers of humanistic psychology, similarly expressed this sentiment in his book "Psychology of Science" (Maslow 1966) by entitling a chapter "The Pathology of Recognition: Anxiety Reducing Mechanisms of Knowledge". In another chapter, we find a list of 21 'pathological' 'primarily anxiety-related' forms which manifest in our need to 'acquire knowledge, to know, and to understand.' A further chapter begins: "Science can, therefore, so serve defense. It can be primarily a philosophy of security, a defense system, a complex tool for avoiding anxiety."

- the most extensive elimination of the unpredictable and uncontrollable,
- the reduction of influencing variables,
- the most extensive prediction of the results of actions,
- maximal control of all things that can happen,
- concealing one's own motives and emotions behind a "correct" methodology,
- restriction of experiences to the region that is pre-defined by those questions and procedures that are considered to be "acceptable" and "permitted".

When we have grasped all of these, what can we do, concretely?

The most important aspect that I wanted to develop here was to argue for the effectiveness of the principles of Humanistic Psychology in opposition to the ideology of an effectiveness based on principles of mechanistic science. To call the latter "scientific" in order to accuse the Humanistic Approach of being "unscientific" is in itself pseudo-scientific and pseudo-factual because it ignores the fact that the so-called "scientific" principles of a mechanistic understanding of interventions became antiquated when viewed from the perspective of modern science. In contrast, the principles of Humanistic Psychology and modern systems science correspond very well (without pleading for a reduction of Humanistic Psychology to natural sciences!).

As a consequence, there is no reason at all to sheepishly apologize for working on the principles of Humanistic Psychology. The incorrectly posed dichotomy of "effective or humanistic" and the misunderstood "scientific bases" of a mechanistic worldview should not make people shut up. Rather, it calls for progressive support of the principles of the Humanistic Approach. In such discussions, we must be prepared for resistance and fear of those who continue to demand "order" and "effective-ness" purely through control and only by means of quan-titative measures of quality[12]. We can, however, be sure of support from the natural sciences. And so we can hope that the effectiveness of the Humanistic Psychological Approach will overcome the contemporary anti-humanis-tic effectiveness that is—together with other absurdities of misunderstood "science"—hostile to human life pro-cesses.

References

Johnson LD, Shaha S (1996): Improving quality in psycho-therapy. Psychotherapy, 33, 225-236

Kriz, J. (1992) Chaos und Struktur. Systemtheorie Bd 1. Mün-chen, Berlin: Quintessenz

Kriz, J. (1993) In der Baumschule. Scheidewege, 23, 1993, Bd II, 432-439

Kriz, J. (1997b): Chaos, Angst und Ordnung. Wie wir unsere Lebenswelt gestalten. Göttingen: Vandenheock

Kriz, J. (1997a) Systemtheorie. Eine Einführung für Psycho-therapeuten, Psychologen und Mediziner. Wien: Facultas

Maslow, A. (1966) The Psychology of Science. New York: Harper & Row

Primas, H. (1995) Über dunkle Aspekte der Naturwissenschaft. In: Atmanspacher, Harald, et al. (Hrsg.): Der Pauli-Jung-Dialog und seine Bedeutung für moderne Wissenschaft. Berlin, Heidelberg: Springer, 205-238

Walter, H.-J. (1985) Gestaltthoerie und Psychotherapie. 2. Aufl. Opladen: Westdeutscher Verlag

---

[12] In spite of some critical discussion that the "quality control" and Quality Assurance (QA) used by managed care organizations do not appear to directly address quality of services and, moreover, factually hinder innovation and more practical measures of outcome (Johnson & Shaha, 1996), this reductive idea of "quality" is increasingly im-posed on psychotherapy.